SCHOOL RENOVATION HANDBOOK

INVESTING IN EDUCATION

Glen I. Earthman, Ed.D.
Virginia Polytechnic Institute and State University

LANCASTER · BASEL

School Renovation Handbook: Investing in Education
a **TECHNOMIC®** publication

Published in the Western Hemisphere by
Technomic Publishing Company, Inc.
851 New Holland Avenue, Box 3535
Lancaster, Pennsylvania 17604 U.S.A.

Distributed in the Rest of the World by
Technomic Publishing AG
Missionsstrasse 44
CH-4055 Basel, Switzerland

Printed in the United States of America
10 9 8 7 6 5 4 3 2 1

Main entry under title:
School Renovation Handbook: Investing in Education

A Technomic Publishing Company book
Bibliography: p.
Includes index p. 179

Library of Congress Catalog Card No. 94-60644
ISBN No. 1-56676-153-0

CONTENTS

INTRODUCTION

IN six short years, as the country enters the twenty-first century, many school buildings will turn 50 years old. The greatest number of school buildings in use today were constructed between 1950 and 1970 in response to the baby boom that followed World War II.

Not only were there a large number of school buildings constructed during this time period, a sizable portion of these buildings were inexpensive structures. The local school board was so interested in housing a growing school age population that the initial cost of the building was the biggest concern; the quality of the building was secondary. In fact, good quality building material was extremely scarce during the first decade following the war, and buildings were constructed with whatever building material was available. In addition, communities were hard pressed to fund the constant building program of the local school system, so initial costs were kept as low as possible. As the buildings of the 1950s and 1960s continue to age, it will become more difficult to house students and educational programs because of structural deficiencies, capacity constraints, and technological limitations. School boards and administrators will be faced with the question of whether to renovate and renew these aging structures or plan new facilities.

Educators and school boards often believe renovating a school building is less expensive and faster than planning, designing, and building a new structure. Such is not the universal case. Each potential renovation project needs to be considered individually. Renovation may not always be the least expensive or the fastest, but it is often the most politically acceptable answer to the situation. The fact that many school systems will consider a renovation project in the immediate future serves as an impetus for this publication. This book will provide a step-by-step approach to the planning process of a renovation, renewal, or modernization project for educators throughout the country.

There are many factors that enter into the decision to renovate a building that are not necessarily considered in constructing a new building. Adverse results may occur during a renovation project that do not usually occur in a new building project; these possible results are considered in this book so that educators can be aware of them before initiating a project. Drawing these factors and results to the attention of educators and school boards may help them in making a decision. Although some of these factors may resemble truisms, they are, nevertheless, items to be considered by the decision makers.

(*1*) Completing a renovation project on an existing building is not like a new building project. There is a difference in the kinds of decisions that are made, the order in which decisions are made, and how data are gathered for the decisions.

(*2*) Renovation project decisions are always difficult to make and are not always decided upon in terms of finances.

(*3*) Preliminary studies in the form of architectural drawings are necessary in assisting in the initial decision-making process.

(*4*) Architects have more constraints to deal with in trying to achieve the needed spaces and relationships in an existing building than in a new building project.

(*5*) Renovation is not always the least expensive way to provide modern educational settings or classroom spaces.

(*6*) The end product of the renovation project may not be as desirable as when initially considered.

(*7*) Renovation projects are difficult for the students and staff of a school going through the process. There is considerable displacement of the educational program.

(*8*) Costs of a renovation project usually increase during the construction phase because of various field conditions. There is a high probability of this happening in every project.

(*9*) With every renovation project there is the strong possibility of encountering asbestos in the building, which means that special precautions must be taken for its removal. This will increase the total cost of the project.

For these reasons, educators should enter into a renovation project with a great deal of caution and an understanding of the process and what problems to anticipate. This book was prepared in an effort to assist educators in making difficult decisions by presenting the planning process in a straightforward manner.

Glen I. Earthman
Virginia Polytechnic Institute and State University

CHAPTER 1

Problems of Maintenance and Renovation

INTRODUCTION

VARIOUS national reports have given a great deal of attention to the state of the educational programs offered by local school systems throughout the United States. At the same time, however, these reports have been strangely silent on the physical condition of the school facilities in which the programs are housed. Further, the remedies specified for ameliorating the problems concerning educational programs have little or nothing to do with improving the condition of the buildings. Understandably, people in all walks of life are more concerned about the effectiveness of an educational program than in the space where the instructional/learning process takes place. Although every parent is interested in the condition of a school's physical environment, and the parents are very vocal when conditions become extreme, these same parents do not press the issue when conditions are only less than desirable. The ability to distinguish acceptable from non-acceptable is more difficult than comparing extremes.

Common knowledge in the field of education dictates that the essence of learning is in having a good teacher and that a good teacher can do an effective job of teaching regardless of where the instruction takes place. Samuel Clemens is credited with saying something to the effect that the ideal educative situation was a student at one end of a log and Mark Hopkins (a great Harvard University professor) at the other end. The idea behind this statement is that a good teacher is all that is needed for a well-rounded education. Unfortunately, many laypersons still believe something similar to that statement. Although no thoughtful educator would subscribe to such simplistic thoughts, the lack of significant concern by educators and school board members to where education takes place gives impetus to the erroneous idea that the physical environment has little or no effect upon the learning process of a student.

Educators who have worked in both excellent and poor facilities can emphatically attest to the need for buildings that adequately support the educational programs that the school system offers. In addition to the empirical evidence from practitioners regarding the effect buildings have upon learners, there are research findings that support the idea that facilities do, in fact, have an impact upon the effectiveness of the instructional program and upon the ability of students to learn (McGuffey, 1982). In reviewing over two decades of research, McGuffey concludes that buildings can indeed affect pupil achievement, even though the amount of variance that can be attributed to the building is small. The total amount of variance accounted for by all school-related factors, at best, is very small; therefore, the variance accounted for by the building takes on increased importance. Over 180 studies were examined by McGuffey to determine the effects school buildings have upon students and educational programs. In a recent study, Cash (1993) found a difference of five percentage points between achievement scores of students in buildings rated above and below standard. A five-percentage-point difference in student scores may at first seem rather insignificant, but it can mean a great deal to the administrator who is trying to raise all student achievement scores. In other words, there may be the possibility of increasing student test scores by increasing funds to improve a facility in which the students are housed. The expenditure of funds may actually result in a higher rate of student learning. The suggested causal relationship between the two variables is tenuous, but significant. Although not conclusive, the results of this study do provide an avenue for speculation and possible action on the part of administrators. A building administrator would be remiss not to take advantage of any such possibility. Cash's study also supports some earlier findings by Chan (McGuffey, 1982) and others who studied the relationship between student achievement and various conditions of buildings. Although there is no conclusive evidence of the relationship between building condition and teacher effectiveness or student achievement, there is enough evidence to make decision makers aware of the importance of insuring that students within their charge are housed in the best facilities the community can afford. The possibility that improving the learning environment by improving the physical facilities, with the result of better student performance, is sufficient to compel school boards and administrators to provide them.

In spite of this evidence, educators are so often forced to house students in facilities that were not designed to fit the program, or that are not even safe or healthy for young people to inhabit. Oftentimes the reason for this is either the inability or the unwillingness of the community to appropriate sufficient funds to provide adequate buildings.

In many parts of the country, poorly designed or run-down buildings serve several generations of students before adequate facilities are made available. In times of rapid educational program change, educators are unable to keep up with the space demands of new programs. Classic examples of this are the attempts by educators to accommodate special education programs in conventional school buildings. Even today it is not uncommon to find the speech therapy program housed in a former closet or the school psychologist testing in a band practice room. These types of accommodations are expedient unfortunately, because the specialist has to overcome the building condition to properly serve students.

In addition to inappropriate space assignment, existing buildings continue to age and require attention. As a result, school systems are usually in a catch-up position as far as providing safe and modern facilities are concerned. National reports have periodically focused on the poor condition of school facilities throughout the nation. The first report of any consequence was done in 1983 under the auspices of the American Association of School Administrators, the Council of Great City Schools, and the National School Boards Association (AASA, 1983). This survey was completed using a sample of 100 randomly selected school systems in 33 states and the District of Columbia. From this sample, the facility maintenance needs of the 15,500 school systems in the country were projected. The report indicated that $25 billion dollars would be needed. This amount represented only the backlog of maintenance needs for school systems and does not include construction costs for new schools to accommodate the natural growth in student population or replacement costs for worn-out school buildings. At the same time, maintenance needs of other parts of the country's infrastructure, such as highways, bridges, dams, airports, mass transit systems, railroads, water and sewer systems, jails, libraries, courts, and public buildings, were being surveyed (AGCA, 1982). The estimate given for the entire backlog of maintenance needs for the entire infrastructure system, including school buildings, was in the neighborhood of $900 billion dollars.

The estimates of the AASA report, as well as the AGCA report, are in 1983 dollars and do not reflect inflation for the interim period of time. Given that this report is now eleven years old, the amount of funds required to complete maintenance needs in school systems in the country may well approach $40 billion dollars, assuming conservative, modest inflation rates.

In 1989, a study on the condition of existing public school buildings throughout the country was published (Educational Writers Association, 1989). This report indicated that approximately $41 billion dollars was needed for deferred maintenance and major repair of existing buildings, and an additional $84 billion was needed for new construction and the retrofit of older buildings, for a total of $125 billion in capital improvement projects. The results of this investigation were not different from the 1983 study, only more current. The same dismal story of maintenance backlogs and lack of funds was told by the EWA report as was told by the earlier AASA report.

The data used in the 1989 analysis were obtained through a survey of state departments of education. The office responsible for school facilities in each state was contacted by the EWA for data regarding condition of school buildings, amount of maintenance funds needed and available, and planning capability of localities. Only twenty eight states and the District of Columbia responded to the survey, resulting in a 55 percent return. A rate of return this low does not ordinarily inspire a great deal of confidence in the results of the study. However, the main thrust of the report was to point out the fact that school buildings need attention.

Although maintenance work in local school systems has been continued during this eleven-year period of time (1983–94), the buildings have not escaped aging and still require further maintenance work. As a result, one might assume that the dollar amount needed for maintenance of the school systems throughout the country is much the same as before, even if specific maintenance projects may differ.

The backlog of maintenance costs, coupled with the fact that by the year 2000 school buildings constructed immediately after World War II and into the 1950s will be fifty years old and in need of major renovation, presents a formidable problem for school boards throughout the country. The normal useful life of a school building is forty to fifty years at which time major renovations and improvements are needed. In a recent national study of the condition of school buildings, it was reported that 30.6 percent of the entire school building inventory of the country was built prior to 1950 and another 21.4 percent before 1959 (AASA, 1991). Additionally, 22.4 percent of the school buildings were constructed in the 1960s. This is a gigantic number of school buildings that are considered old. Conversely, only 11.2 percent of the school buildings in the country were built since 1980. Due to the fuel crisis of 1973, schools constructed in 1973 and beyond were designed with many energy-conserving features. Unfortunately, the more efficiently designed school buildings only make up a small percentage (11.2) of all functioning school buildings.

Many of the post-World War II buildings, and even those built as late as the early 1970s, were hurriedly constructed to meet the burgeoning student enrollments. These buildings in many instances were poorly constructed, frequently with inferior building material, because good quality material was often not available. In addition, many school boards at that time were more interested in keeping the initial cost of buildings as low as possible than they were in the construction of high-quality buildings. The result was an abundance of poor-quality school buildings which have not stood up well against the onslaught of, in some cases, half a century's use. As these buildings age, decisions regarding their future will have to be made. Problems such as out-of-date boilers, limited electrical load systems, primitive air-conditioning systems, limited plumbing systems, weakened superstructures, and the inevitable leaking roof will have to be addressed when deciding whether or not these buildings are to serve students and communities in the future, and if so, how they would be used.

Concurrent with this, the amount of funds devoted to maintenance work in the local school system has declined over the years. In looking at the proportion of local school budgets devoted to maintenance from 1920 to 1982, the National Center for Education Statistics reported that the percentage has declined by 7.4 percent (1982). In 1920, 14.1 percent of the local school budget was devoted to maintenance work; however, the percentage for 1982 was 6.7 percent. There are several reasons that explain the precipitous drop in maintenance funds over this sixty-two-year period. Most of the reasons center around the limited financial resources available to the school system and the competing budget demands of other local governmental units, the constantly changing student enrollment in the schools, high energy costs, and the age of buildings in the inventory of the school system. When the local school boards reduce the maintenance portion of the proposed budget to balance it, there are few or no parents or teachers demanding that the cut be restored. Such budget reductions become increasingly easy for school boards when there are no factions in the school system that fight the reduction. Regardless of the circumstances or reasons for the reduction, the fact remains that over the past sixty-two years, the amount of funds devoted to maintenance, repair, and upkeep of school buildings has noticeably diminished, while at the same time, the number of school buildings in service has substantially increased.

The AASA conducted another national study of school facilities and energy use in 1991 (AASA). The study was a compilation of existing data on school buildings, finance, school energy, and environmental concerns, and a formulation of the results. As part of the nation-wide study, data from a survey conducted by Educational Research Service were used. This survey drew a random sample of 2,418 elementary and secondary school administrators as respondents. The administrators replied to a survey instrument regarding the condition of the building in which they were located and the reasons for their estimation. The report details several critical issues that confront public schools:

- The school building inventory of this country is aging. Many of the buildings are structurally unsound and environmentally unsafe.
- Many of the school buildings are not safe for students to inhabit.
- The indoor environments of the schools pose a problem to educators who have little guidance in facilities management.
- Financial resources of the local school system are extremely limited.
- The concern for energy conservation in school buildings is not a high-priority item.
- There is a federal and state void in leadership in helping the local school system with facility problems.

The conclusions indicate the condition of school facilities and the degree of leadership exercised in maintaining this community investment.

The investment in school buildings that America has made over the many decades and in some cases centuries, represents a substantial amount of capital. Some people estimate the cost of replacing the existing inventory at something in excess of $3 trillion. The country simply could not afford to replace all of the schools now in operation, yet in many communities, the school buildings are rapidly deteriorating with very little effort made to stop the decline. One reason for this is a general lack of positive action to mount a first class maintenance program to bring the existing schools up to original condition. School board members, educators, and even community members do not take the necessary, positive steps to raise taxes to properly maintain these buildings. Another reason is new, competing demands for each dollar in the school budget. All of this is in the face of a constantly aging building inventory. The largest part of the inventory constructed prior to the 1960s will be fifty years old at the turn of the century, less than six years away. Many of these buildings are of marginal quality, so the school board is presented with the problem of what to do with the inadequate facilities. In addition, in an era of limited funds, maintenance funds have been reduced for the past two to three decades to balance the local school budget. The resulting deferred maintenance has accelerated the deterioration of existing buildings.

SCHOOL BOARD RESPONSIBILITY

All school boards are charged either by law or policy to keep the physical facilities of the school system in good repair. Above and beyond these laws and policies, school boards have a moral responsibility to preserve the investment of the local community in public buildings. These buildings are a public trust held by the school board for the community. School boards readily accept this moral and legal responsibility in the name of the community. As such, the school board directs the administration to organize itself so as to insure that the buildings are kept in good repair. School boards then provide funds to actually mount a program designed to do just that.

Many activities are included under the general rubric of maintenance. Both short-term and long-term maintenance actions are beneficial to all buildings. Some of the projects are rather small, such as replacing a light bulb or a tile on the floor, and some are major tasks that concern very basic systems of the structure. Obviously some of the minor tasks can be completed by a custodian in a matter of minutes, and others are costly and time-consuming.

Regardless of the size of the job, the cost, and the time needed to complete it, all of these activities go towards keeping the building in good shape. Some legal provisions mandate that certain projects be paid for with certain funds and bid in certain ways. In addition, state law and common practice tend to codify certain projects or activities in specified ways. The remainder of this chapter will address each of the terminologies used in this field—maintenance, renovation, renewal, modernization, rehabilitation, and preventative maintenance.

MAINTENANCE

Maintenance consists of those actions which will help to keep a building in a state of good repair, functioning properly, and as near as possible to the condition it was in when it was first constructed. These actions or projects range from painting to repairing walls, to re-roofing, to boiler or window replacement. Most of such activities, in the classical sense, do not enhance the structure beyond the point of what the original building contained.

Maintenance projects can be classified into four major groups: (1) long-range maintenance, (2) annual projects, (3) short-term periodic maintenance, and (4) emergency maintenance or repairs. Each maintenance program includes all of the above kinds of projects at some time or other. In fact, the maintenance schedules of larger school systems include all of these categories each year. Some projects such as replacing lighting fixtures, pointing the brick work outside the building, and boiler replacement are examples of long-term maintenance projects. Some of these projects can be funded from capital funds. The annual projects usually deal with items noted from an annual inspection and deal with projects such as reconditioning of floors, painting, and minor repairs on machinery. The short-term, periodic maintenance projects cover those items required to keep machinery in good condition, such as oiling and greasing, providing minor tune-ups to motors, and keeping door hardware in good working condition. Items in the last category deal with emergency conditions such as a broken window, a clogged toilet, or a door that will not operate. These items cannot be planned for, except by having procedures for coping with an emergency.

Major maintenance activities can be contrasted to those actions which serve to repair parts of the building by restoring systems or parts of buildings to their original condition. Repairing parts of a building is a very important and worthwhile function and keeps the structure in good condition so that the users can function in a healthy and safe environment, but usually repair items are small in nature and result from some failure of a system or structure. Of course, the results of natural disasters can result in rather large repair items such as replacing a roof or other parts of structures. Repair items, however, are not planned for as are maintenance items and result from emergency situations.

RENOVATION

Renovation usually refers to those actions involved in changing and improving the physical environment of a building. These activities are implemented to improve the structure as well as the space within the building. The maintenance of a building may include a series of actions designed to keep the building in good order, but these items may or may not be related to each other and may be accomplished over a period of years. There may not be a conscientious effort to coordinate all of the improvements to a building under a maintenance schedule. In renovating a building, however, all of the items that are included in the project are coordinated to bring the building up to a certain standard, which has been determined by the school administration, within a specified period of time.

Renovation usually involves major renewal of utility systems within the building, in addition to a change of space within the structure, and perhaps exterior work. Renovation projects may be partial or complete and the difference is in the inclusiveness of the items within the project. For example, a partial renovation of a building may include renewal of several, but not all, of the major utility systems and no change of space within the structure. A complete renovation would include a renewal of all of the utility systems and some structural changes, such as a new roof or changes in space.

The difference between the three states of repair of a building—maintenance, partial renovation, and complete renovation—is really a matter of completeness or inclusiveness. The maintenance of a building is a continuous process involving many items and projects that may or may not be related. A partial renovation includes projects of system renewal that are related to each other and are completed within a specified period of time. The complete renovation renews all of the utility systems, structural elements, and space within the building in one project, completed within a specified period of time. The elements of inclusiveness and time are important in trying to delineate between the three terms. Maintenance items or projects may and usually are included under a renovation program. Likewise, projects usually included in a renovation can be included in a maintenance program.

To confound the issue even more is the fact that educators use other terms to describe various degrees of improvement of the existing school building. Words such as renewal, modernization, and rehabilitation are frequently used, sometimes interchangeably, to describe the actions taken to improve the building to the point where it has the same systems and spaces as the newest building in the school system. Such substitution causes confusion and necessitates a definition of the term to allow persons to communicate effectively.

Funds for repair items come from the same section of the budget as do funds for maintenance items—the operational budget of the school system. In every state, the local school system budget contains a section devoted to maintenance and operations. In this section, funds are lodged to pay for craftsmen employed by the school system who will work on both maintenance and repair items. In many cases, the same personnel who complete the repair items also do some maintenance work. In this respect, maintenance and repair are no different from each other. The only difference might be in the manner in which repair items are requested and disposed. As stated above, repair needs usually stem from emergency situations and must be taken care of immediately. The burst water pipe cannot wait for budgetary considerations by the school board. Neither can the water faucet that leaks. Additionally, the broken window must be repaired immediately to prevent further damage to structure and content. All of these situations need immediate attention to bring the building back to its original condition and to prevent further damage. The reporting of these items is usually done by phone or fax, not through the usual mail routes, and the repair is completed as soon as possible.

RENEWAL

Some school systems use the term "renewal" to describe what is done to a building to improve it and bring it up-to-date with the most modern, similar building in the system. Renewal includes improvements which are done in a complete renovation. In fact the two terms are usually interchangeable in practice. Renewal is probably the better word for a project that completely overhauls a building in every respect, preparing it to accommodate a modern educational program, and providing it with all of the environmental comforts needed for students to properly learn and for teachers to effectively teach. A partial renovation project can improve some, but not all, of the utility systems, such as replacement of wooden windows or roof. A complete renovation or renewal project would improve every mechanical and structural system, plus change spaces to accommodate newer educational programs. This seems to be the difference between renewal and some renovation applications. In this text, however, complete renovation means the same as renewal or modernization and includes a comprehensive overhaul of the building.

REHABILITATION

This term is usually reserved for completion of those improvements which would normally would have been completed under a regularly funded maintenance program. Rehabilitation includes those maintenance items which were left undone or deferred in previous years. In other words, the deferred maintenance items are usually the basis of a rehabilitation project.

PREVENTATIVE MAINTENANCE

Many school systems have in operation a program for systematically servicing various motors and equipment in the schools to prevent premature failure. Included in a preventative maintenance program are an inventory of all operating motors and equipment, the type of service needed for each, and the schedule of routine check-ups for each so that proper attention can be given on a regular basis. The objective of preventative maintenance programs is to assure that every working part of the building is in good order and to prevent failure before expected. Such attention does in fact extend the normal life of operating motors and equipment.

A preventative maintenance program could also address structures and systems of the building. A regular painting schedule for a building extends the life of the building itself and is a routinely scheduled effort which can be included under the general definition of preventative maintenance. Replacement of certain parts of the building could also be included in a preventative maintenance program. Some school systems have programs that call for the replacement of a roof or boiler, for instance, at the end of a pre-determined useful life. Replacement of machinery or parts of a building on a pre-determined date can have many advantages over emergency measures. Such replacement can be propitiously timed to prevent interruption of the educational program, and to occur when funds are available.

For many years, school systems have used preventative measures to safeguard the useful life of machines and equipment. In addition, school systems have systematically employed practices which retard deterioration and keep the building in prime condition. The extent of these preventative practices and measures varies a great deal throughout the country. Regardless of the definition or extent of preventative maintenance programs, such efforts pay off handsomely for the school system by preventing (1) lost school time of teachers and students; (2) accompanying damage to other parts of the structure; (3) high cost of replacement during an emergency; and (4) negative impact upon the remainder of the maintenance program. Further, preventative maintenance programs can in many instances extend the useful life of parts of a building.

REFERENCES

AASA. 1983. *The Maintenance Gap: Deferred Repair and Renovation in the Nation's Elementary and Secondary Schools.* Arlington, VA: A Joint Report by the American Association of School Administrators, Council of Great City Schools, and National School Board Association.

Associated General Contractors of America. 1982. *Fractured Framework: Why America Must Rebuild.* The Association.

Cash, C. 1993. "Building Conditions and Student Achievement and Behavior," Unpublished dissertation. Virginia Polytechnic Institute and State University.

Educational Writers Association. 1989. *Wolves at the Schoolhouse Door: An Investigation of the Condition of Public School Buildings.* Washington, D.C.: The Association.

McGuffey, C. 1982. "Facilities," Chapter 10, H. Walberg, ed., *Improving Educational Standards and Productivity.* McCutchan Publishing Co.

National Center for Educational Statistics. 1982. *Digest of Education Statistics, 1982.* Washington, D.C.: NCES.

CHAPTER 2

Decision to Renovate

INTRODUCTION

WHEN increased student enrollments exceed the building capacity of the school system, the decision to plan and construct a new school building is easier to make than the decision to renovate, renew, or modernize an existing building. Student growth beyond the limit of existing capacity is easily determined and relief in the form of new construction is readily supported. The decision to construct a new building is not necessarily easy to make because it means the school system will need to go into long-term debt to pay it. Other difficult decisions relate to the size of the building and its location. Although the myriad of questions that need to be answered in constructing a new school are vexing and difficult, the line of action is relatively straightforward, and the school board and administration can feel easily justified in making the decision to build a new school. This is not so in deciding what action, if any, to take to improve an existing building.

There are many frequently used terms related to improving an existing school building, including "rehabilitation," "renovation," "remodeling," "renewal," and "modernization." Many times these terms are used interchangeably. All these words deal with some sort of improvement, and the difference is probably more in the degree of improvement than in any esoteric definition.

Rehabilitation often refers to the action of restoring the building to its original condition, which is what the regular maintenance program should do. Where deferred maintenance has been practiced for a period of time, school systems must make a bootstrap effort to rehabilitate buildings by completing all of the deferred work. Rehabilitation is often preventative maintenance work that is completed in order for the building to be restored to its original condition. Most of the rehabilitation is cosmetic in nature and the major utility services and structure are usually not changed.

Remodeling is more extensive than rehabilitation, but not as extensive as other processes. Remodeling may apply to only one area in the school or it may include a complete change or improvement. Remodeling also refers to changes in space and sometimes to changes in location of functions. There is usually the implication of some physical change in wall configuration. Major utility systems may or may not be included in a remodeling project.

The terms "renovation," "renewal," and "modernization" are usually synonymous. Each of these words describes what is done to a building to completely overhaul the systems and bring it up to the condition of the most modern building in the school system. Always included in renovation, renewal, and modernization projects are improvements in all of the utility systems, plus physical changes to the structure. Appendix B contains a list of items that can be completed in renewal projects for elementary, middle, and high school buildings.

The decision to renovate an existing building does not lend itself to an easy solution because there are so many confounding variables to consider before a decision can be made. The cost of renovation or renewal is not the only factor that must be examined. School boards and administrators must be aware of other factors and handle them with a great deal of sensitivity and rationality.

There are many reasons for renovating, renewing, or modernizing an existing building. Most of the time school buildings are obsolete long before their useful life is reached. Such buildings are prime candidates for a renovation or renewal so that they can properly support the current educational program. Some school systems find it important to renovate or renew a school building once it has reached a pre-determined age of existence, such as twenty years. There may be some variations on these two major motivating factors, but basically they are the primary reasons for scheduling such a project.

Renovation or renewal may be the initial choice of the school board when confronted with either constructing a new building or renovating an existing one, because of the general perception that renovation represents the lowest initial cost and earliest occupancy. Unfortunately there is no simple rule of thumb that can be used to assist in making that decision. Guidelines, based upon experience, have been suggested to provide help in arriving at a decision; however, guidelines or rules alone never take into consideration all of the factors that need to be considered. Linn (1952) suggests that the decision to modernize or renovate a building is probably questionable if the cost of modernization exceeds 50 percent of the cost of a new project. According to Linn, a lower figure, such as 40 percent of the cost of replacement, would be more appropriate.

Another formula that was developed by Castaldi has been widely used in the school planning process. The Castaldi Generalized Formula for School Modernization seeks to estimate costs on the basis of the major components of modernization, namely, the cost of educational, health, and safety improvements, plus site considerations (Castaldi, 1994). The formula considers a rate of depreciation and uses an hypothesis which has depreciation as the determinant. The rate of depreciation represents the amount of funds needed to provide facilities that are adequate in every phase. Modernization is justifiable if:

$$\frac{(Ce + Ch + Cs)}{(Lm)\,(Ia)} < \frac{R}{Lr}$$

where

Ce = Total cost of educational improvements
Ch = Total cost for improvements in healthfulness (physical, aesthetic, and psychological)
Cs = Total cost for improvements in safety
Ia = Estimated index of educational adequacy (0 – 1)
Lm = Estimated useful life of the modernized school
R = Cost of replacement of school considered for modernization
Lr = Estimated life of new building (Castaldi, 1994)

The total cost of educational improvements (*Ce*) will include additions to the building as well as the site, special wiring for electronic technology, and even new furniture and equipment. The cost for improvements for health purposes (*Ch*) might include such items as refenestration, air conditioning, resurfacing of floors, and upgrading the toilets. The cost for improvements in safety (*Cs*) would include making structural repairs, fireproofing stairways, repairing ceilings and roofs, and fencing for the school yard.

The "*Ia*" in the formula is an index of educational adequacy, or how well the building and site accommodates the educational program. This is a subjective evaluation of how well the structure provides spaces that are needed by students and teachers for modern teaching/learning processes. This judgment must be made by educators, but the evaluation should be made by educators both inside and outside the school system from proposed architectural plans and not from the actual renovated building itself. An architect must first review the educational program determined by the school system to draw up plans, which in turn are evaluated by the educators to see if the suggested changes will work properly. This type of evaluation is no different than what an educator does when reviewing plans for a new building. Basically, the educator projects a program into a proposed facility. The indeterminate factor is whether or not some condition in the existing building will prevent the creation of desired space arrangements.

"*Lm*" represents the estimated number of years of useful life of the building after renovation. This judgment is also rather subjective; it should be based upon the best possible evidence and probably should be made by the architect or engineer. The evaluation should take into consideration the structural elements of the building as well as its capacity for further changes to its internal spaces.

The symbols *R* and *Lr* indicate the cost of a new school building to replace the older one and the number of years the new building would be in use. It is assumed that maintenance costs of renovated and new buildings would be the same for the expected life of both. This may not actually be the case because a newer, well-constructed building would undoubtedly require less maintenance than a renovated building would over the life of the buildings.

This formula can be used successfully to compare renovation versus new construction by supplying appropriate data. Castaldi compares his formula with that of Linn on a hypothetical building and concludes that the Linn formula is a special case of the Generalized Formula; however, the results of the two different methods probably would not concur for a school building less than forty-five years of age. Both of these formulae are very useful in attempting to quantify a very difficult decision. Each formula provides the school board with a numerical comparison of renovation or renewal and construction of a new facility. This precision adds a degree of definitiveness to the decision-making process.

There are some problems with the Generalized Formula for School Modernization, just as there are for many hypothetical formulae. In the case of the Generalized Formula, one problem is the difficulty in separating out those renovations items that can be ascribed to educational program needs as opposed to health and safety factors. For example, installing carpet in the library could be either an educational program improvement or a safety improvement. The same could be said for replacement of windows. Even if there is general agreement on the separation of various improvements into the three categories, there is still a certain amount of subjectivity in the formula when an educator must estimate the extent of the facility's educational adequacy. This estimate must rely upon the professional judgment of an educator after a review of proposed architectural plans.

Such problems with the formula do not in any way suggest that it is less than adequate for assisting in providing data to decision makers, because these formulae do provide a measure of comparison between two sets of action. But the problems in the application of either formula do point out rather vividly the entire subjective nature of the decision to renovate an existing building.

Mathematical formulae, however, do not necessarily provide all of the data the school board needs to make decisions regarding the possibility of renovation; the use of these formulae without other data confound the situation and make the decision more difficult because the results of the formulae can be used to prove almost anything. Cost of the project is, of course, a consideration in making the decision. It is not, however, the *sine qua non* of the decision. School boards do, unfortunately, rely heavily on the total cost of any project in making a decision. There are some basic factors that should be evaluated when a renovation or renewal project is under consideration:

- educational program requirements
- flexibility to accommodate new teaching methods
- educational technology requirements
- compliance with life safety and handicap codes
- architectural upgrading
- asbestos abatement and other environmental requirements
- thermal efficiency of the building environment
- adequacy and efficiency of mechanical and electrical systems
- adequacy of present site
- site modification requirements
- availability of school building construction
- schedule requirements
- current construction market
- historical, emotional, and political issues

These factors are a combination of many different facets of the problem. Most of these factors can be regrouped into four rather large topics: the school building itself, the site, the costs, and the political/emotional issues. The following facilities questions can be grouped as such:

(*1*) School building adaptability and condition
- How well can the building accommodate new educational programs?
- Can any and all utility systems be successfully upgraded?
- Can the building be changed to comply with handicap needs and regulations?
- Is there sufficient thermal efficiency of the building envelope?
- Is the building sufficiently attractive and architecturally interesting to warrant preservation through renovation or renewal?

(*2*) School site
- Is it large enough to accommodate a modern program?
- Is there sufficient usable space?
- Is the site located near where students live?
- Is there suitable transportation available?
- Is a site for a new school readily available?

(*3*) Financial considerations
- What is the cost/benefit ratio of renovating?
- Is the renovation cost effective?
- What is the comparison between renovation and new construction costs?

(*4*) Political and emotional issues
- Is the decision to renovate acceptable to the power structure and community?
- Are there emotional issues tied to renovating a building?
- Is there a particular community attachment to a building which would influence the decision?

This four-part analysis, which is often suggested by architects, should be completed before a decision on renovation is made. This chart lists the four categories of analysis, the specific data needed under each category, and the party responsible for gathering data. The owner in this situation would be the staff representing the school board, and the architect/engineer is the outside expertise employed by the school system, if the school system does not possess that expertise on the staff. If the school system is sufficiently large enough, both architectural and engineering expertise are employed by the school system. School systems often employ educational consultants to assist the school staff in gathering data for the decision. An educational consultant can provide a degree of objectivity, in addition to expertise, for the interpretation of the data.

Four-Step Evaluation Critical to Renovation Projects

Type of Evaluation	Components	Performed by
1. Technical survey of the facility	Arch/struct condition	A/E
	Code deficiencies	A/E
	HVAC/electrical	A/E
	Site conditions	A/E
	Operating and maintenance cost	Owner
	Historic	A/E
2. Analysis of institution's education objectives	Meets educational program?	Owner
	Adaptability to future use	A/E:Owner
	Other possible uses	A/E; Owner
3. Financial audit	Convert options into costs	Owner
	Include relocation contingencies	Owner
	Evaluate operating costs	Owner
	Compare to new construction	Owner
4. Examination of political climate	Predisposition of admin	Owner
	Historical/sentimental value	Owner
	Fund-raising potential	Owner
	Preference for status quo versus state-of-the-art	Owner

The first step in the evaluation will produce concrete data concerning the physical condition of a building under consideration for renovation. This step must also be completed, or well underway, to accomplish the other steps effectively. Once it has been determined that a renovation is feasible and will result in a facility that can better accommodate both the educational program and the student population, questions of cost and political climate can be addressed. Assessment of the existing building provides a factually supported basis from which administrators, faculty, school board members, and the community can form an intelligent opinion.

Assessment of a building for renovation possibilities is different from the type of assessment that is carried out for maintenance purposes. In developing the maintenance schedule for the school system, every school building is normally assessed to determine what work needs to be done to return the building to its original condition. This type of assessment really identifies those items that need repair and/or improvement.

Proper assessment of a building is always important when making decisions regarding how students will be housed in school buildings. The purpose and use of the assessment data oftentimes determines when the appraisal is to be done. In the situation where maintenance items are to be identified for funding next year, the appraisal is done every year and many small as well as large items may be identified. In more extensive remodeling projects, the evaluation may be at a specified time, but the items identified as needing work may be limited. In renovation projects, the appraisal of the building is done early in the decision-making stage so that the resultant data can be used to determine whether or not to proceed with the project long before funds are allocated. This difference in time as to when the appraisal is completed demonstrates the uniqueness of the renovation process.

FEASIBILITY STUDIES

In completing an assessment for consideration of a renovation project, the main thrust of the evaluation is to determine the feasibility of renovation, not necessarily to identify those items that would restore the building to its original condition or keep it in good working order. The feasibility study then must look at how well a given educational program can fit into the building after renovation. In addition, the condition of the utility systems and structure need to be assessed during this time. This kind of assessment must provide data upon which a final decision can be made to either proceed or change options.

The preliminary design review under a feasibility study will provide some conceptual ideas and sufficient analyses to estimate the costs of the conditions and requirements that will influence the total price of the renovations. One of the primary uses for these preliminary studies is to identify any potential problems that would generate additional costs when the renovation is in progress. These hidden problems and associated costs oftentimes limit the cost effectiveness of renovation or new construction. Unfortunately, the total cost of a renovation is not known until the project is either well underway or completed. Feasibility studies will, however, focus the educators on how the educational program can be implemented in the renovated building rather than on the cost of the renovation. If a renovation project is presented to the voters in the form of a bond referendum, the educators will have a stronger position if they can demonstrate how the new, improved educational program will work in the renovated building. This can go a long way in convincing the voters to support the renovation of an older structure.

There are many constraints within an existing building that could prevent an architect from providing the required number of spaces, the right size of spaces, and the proper relationships in a preliminary design for the structure. These constraints may be in the form of load-bearing walls, exterior perimeter of the building, hidden utility lines and services that were not identified before the project started, and present location of specially designed facilities. Even the site could be a constraint if the school building needs expansion to implement the educational program. Unless these constraints are identified early in the project, making a decision to proceed with a renovation can be very difficult and costly and might be less than desirable for the educational program. Preliminary surveys and design reviews may provide some early data that can address the feasibility of the suggested renovation.

The starting point of any assessment of an existing building is to establish the educational program that will be implemented in the structure. This must be done by the educators before the project is initiated. Once the educational program is translated into required spaces and relationships, the architect and engineer can begin to make an evaluation of the building. This program forms the basis of the assessment done by architects and engineers.

EVALUATION PROCESS

The evaluation of a building must be an orderly process designed to produce the types and kinds of data needed for decision making. The office or person responsible for the evaluation should establish a team and develop a process immediately upon notification of the possibility of a renovation project. Usually the person responsible for this task is located in the school facilities department, if such a department exists in the school system. In a rather small school system, this person could well be the coordinator, supervisor, or director of maintenance and operations. If such is the case, that person must organize the effort, call upon other offices in the school system to assist in the study, and secure the services of whatever kind of outside consultants are needed.

If the school system is rather large, architectural expertise is usually employed on the staff. Normally these architects have other review responsibilities and do not have the time to actually assume complete responsibility for a thorough architectural study. In such cases, and in almost every small school system, outside architectural assistance will have to be secured to do the preliminary study. Securing architectural assistance can be accomplished in a number of ways which are outlined in succeeding chapters. Even for the preliminary architectural drawings, however, an architect with experience in renovation should be employed because the experience will enable that person to see possibilities for housing needed programs that an inexperienced architect might not.

The architect should be supported by engineering competence as needed. Such competence may include structural, electrical, plumbing, and heating/ventilation/air-conditioning personnel. The architect and engineers form a design team that actually produces the preliminary study. This kind of review is usually an in-house process designed to produce data, not necessarily solutions. The study results may eventually turn into architectural solutions for the project, following intense review and scrutiny by the staff.

The actual data gathering by the design team consists of studies of the original architectural drawings and any amendments, followed by site visits as needed to insure precise measurements and to check on field conditions. So many times the difference between what was constructed and the architectural drawings used to build the structure is rather amazing. During these site visits, the architect and engineers must verify the measurements of the original drawings and determine the conditions inside the building as well as on the exterior of the structure. These site visits can help the architect determine where utilities are actually located and whether or not the utility services are as stated on the drawings. New drawings must be made where variances between the actual building and the drawings exist.

Selecting the best course of action is a complex assignment for many administrators. In most cases, the options available to decision makers are as varied as the accompanying price tag. On one end of the spectrum, the owner can decide not to make any changes for the time being; the other end is to demolish the structure and build a new facility in its place. In between these two extremes are a number of potential solutions.

After completing the evaluation of the facility, all potential solutions are considered. The design consultant may prepare multiple design concepts, including cost estimates, for the owner. The correct design solution is the one that best suits the institution after all of the available options have been considered. If the priorities and choices are clearly mapped out, the owner can weigh all the variables and come up with the most achievable solution.

Answers to these questions will go a long way in assisting the school board in making a decision to renovate an existing building rather than to raze or abandon it to construct a new one. The solution, however, must pass the muster of acceptance by all parties concerned. Oftentimes the political question is the one that drives the solution more than any other factor, except for cost.

The suggestion by Linn that the cost of renovation should not exceed 50 percent of the cost of replacement of the school and that 40 percent would be a more acceptable limit assumes cost is the only basis for decisions. True, cost is a great motivator in decision making, but to apply that formula, one has to assume that the outcome of the renovation will produce a building capable of adequately accommodating the desired educational program on a site that is large enough to contain the necessary playing fields and parking, and that the final outcome will be acceptable to all concerned. If all of these assumptions are true, then the application of this formula would certainly provide the school board with important data for the decision.

Some of the factors identified above are not susceptible to analysis by producing hard data. For example, how well a building can adjust to fit a new educational program is a matter for the professional judgment of an educator, albeit a subjective judgment. Some of the most important questions are subjective and depend upon the political determination. The following questions from the previous list are ones that can be answered by subjective judgments of educational professionals:

(*1*) How well can the building accommodate new educational programs?

(2) Is the building sufficiently attractive and architecturally interesting to warrant renovation?
(3) Is there sufficient usable space on the site?
(4) Is there suitable public transportation available in the community?
(5) Is the decision to renovate acceptable to the power structure and the community?
(6) Are there emotional issues tied to renovating the building?
(7) Is there a particular community attachment to the building which would influence the decision?

These questions can be answered only by using the best professional judgments of the school board, staff, and any outside educational consultants. The last three questions dealing with community attitudes require a community analysis of some sort to produce data. This analysis can be very informal and the school board itself can make an assessment, or it can be a formal data-gathering approach using community assessment instruments. School boards can have the staff prepare a questionnaire regarding the disposition of a school building. Caution has to be observed in completing such surveys because the community can quickly become solidified in opposing the school board position. The formalization of the data gathering process may be advantageous for gathering unemotional community attitudes. When emotions are strong in the community at least the school system is cognizant of that fact and can develop a program of public relations to provide data for re-consideration by the community. Sometimes informal data gathering by principals and teaching staff may produce a better picture of what the community may be thinking.

Some educators have successfully developed formulae to assist school boards in making a decision to renovate or construct new facilities. In a way this is an attempt to make the decision making more objective by introducing quantifiable data into the process. As laudable as this is, sometimes the final decision is a political one, or is at least based upon some question that may or may not have much to do with the educational program. The number of variables that may be in existence in any situation are so many, it is almost impossible to generalize from one location to another. The unavailability of an adequate site may be sufficient cause to renovate an existing building regardless of how close the cost is to new construction. This applies to other conditions where the options open to the school board concerning renovating are so slight, the actual cost of renovation is a secondary consideration. This must always be kept in mind when examining a situation where both the options of renovation of an existing building and construction of a new facility are available to the school board for consideration.

REFERENCES

Castaldi, B. 1994. *Educational Facilities: Planning, Modernization, and Management. 4th Edition.* Boston: Allyn and Bacon. p. 379.

Linn, H. 1952. "Modernizing School Buildings," *American School and University,* 24:401.

CHAPTER 3

Organizing the Staff for Renovation Projects

INTRODUCTION

ALL organizations, including school systems, need rules and regulations to guide people in working towards the goals of the organization. This means there is some mechanism in place whereby people in the organization are assigned certain tasks or areas of work and given the responsibility and authority to complete them. This division of work and responsibility usually is decided upon by governing or organizational policies. In the public school system the mechanism would be school board policies. These policies divide the work of the school system into various departments throughout the organization. Further, these policies assign certain responsibilities to certain people and also stipulate the manner in which the work is to be completed.

In a simple organization with a limited number of employees or in a single entrepreneurship, these policies may be rudimentary and informal. In contrast, complex organizations, where hundreds and even thousands of people are employed, these policies are extensive and complicated, yet necessary to insure an orderly completion of tasks. Regardless of the size and type of organization, policies are needed to give employees direction and responsibility, as well as authority.

School systems are considered public organizations and as such are governed by many more local, state, and federal laws, rules, ordinances, and regulations than private businesses or organizations. Further, school systems deal with public rights of citizens and subsequently are subject to federal constitutional regulations as defined through court decisions that delineate how the organization is to treat individuals. The public nature of the school system also mandates how employees are treated. All of these considerations must be incorporated into local school board policies, which makes them more extensive than those of the private sector.

SCHOOL BOARD POLICIES

School board policies serve to organize and define the entire staff into the unified scheme of operation needed to accomplish the goals of the organization. These policies not only spell out how the school system will be organized, but also what the specific responsibilities for each segment of the organization are. Therefore, each department within the school system is governed by the policies that are germane to its scope of work. In this manner, the scope of responsibilities for each segment of the organization has a legitimate status through the adopted school board policies.

The department responsible for school facilities is located in the organization of the school system through the school board policies and organizational chart (Figure 3.1). This line and staff chart provides the whole school system with an idea of where responsibility for school facilities lies. In addition, in very large and complex school systems, knowledge of responsibility by everyone in the organization is obtained only through such charts and policy descriptions.

The work of each department, program, and unit of the school system is also set forth in the school board policies. Certain safeguards are built into the policies to insure that the public is being served as efficiently and effectively as possible. For instance, certain goods, supplies, and services are publicly tendered for bid to obtain competitive prices. The manner in which the school system may conduct the bidding process is set forth in the school board policies so that everyone in the school system and in the community knows how the school system will conduct the bid. The department responsible for this task completes the bidding process in exactly the manner prescribed by policy. In this way the school system is fair to everyone who wishes to provide goods and services, it also lets the vendors know they will be treated fairly.

School board policies serve to discourage or eliminate inappropriate behavior by staff members who are dealing with situations where persons outside the organization receive contracts for goods or services. These policies guide the actions of school employees in their contacts with vendors of various sorts. This protects both the school system and the employee.

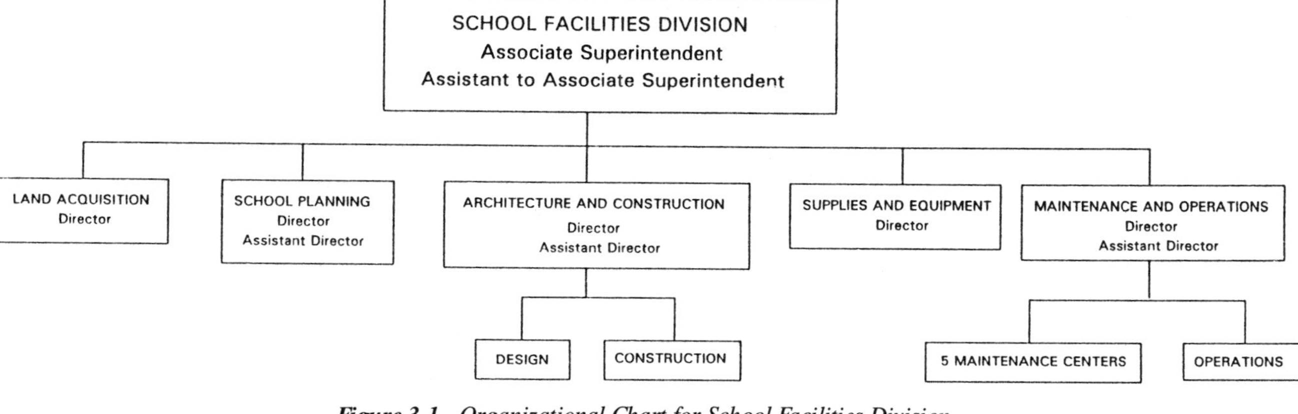

Figure 3.1. *Organizational Chart for School Facilities Division.*

School board policy also covers curriculum change. The procedure for curriculum change usually involves certain specified groups and individuals both inside and outside of the school system. The types and kinds of submissions and approvals of curricular material are also covered under board policy. Such definition of tasks through organizational policy is not uncommon in the public school organization.

SCHOOL MAINTENANCE POLICIES

The employees working in those departments that are responsible for the physical plant of the school system are governed by many general school board policies, but also by those that specifically address the facilities the school system owns and operates. Because of these policies, the school facilities department function impinges upon almost every other department and unit of the school system.

In maintaining and renovating school buildings, certain specific policies must be in evidence to define the responsibility and authority for providing safe, modern facilities. These policies deal with how school buildings are maintained, how renovations and modernization occur, the basis for decisions, and procedures that apply to these activities. Even the establishment of a school building renewal program is addressed by school board policies. The most effective way to mount a systematic renewal of all school buildings is to have a school board policy directive. Such a policy leaves nothing to argument or guesswork and the task becomes something to which the school board and school staff are committed. If such a policy is in place, the question of whether or not to renew a school building is not open for discussion, and capacious action by staff or school board members is prevented. Furthermore as a result of formalizing the renewal program through school board policy funds are more readily dedicated.

In addition to detailing the general organizational structure and assigning responsibility, school board policies also detail certain work that is particular to the maintenance and construction functions of the school system. There are many school board policies that are specific to the school facilities department, but which are not germane to the maintenance and renovation functions of the department. For example, there are usually policy statements governing site acquisition and school building planning and development that might not apply to a renovation project. Such is the case in a policy statement concerning the naming of a new school building. Conceivably, during a renovation project of an existing school, the name of the building might be changed and this policy would come into play, but for the most part, this happens rarely.

General policies of the school system that do apply to maintenance and renovation projects would be in the area of planning, procurement of goods and services, costing of projects, developing educational specifications, determining school capacity, school boundaries, school size, and design, and submittals. Policy statements covering these topics usually refer to new school construction, but nevertheless apply to maintenance and renovation projects. Basic policies that are needed to establish scope of work and responsibility might be the following, which were included in the York County(Va.) School Division School Board policies:

CHAPTER 6
PLANNING AND MAINTAINING THE SCHOOL'S PHYSICAL PLANT

Section 6.1 – General.

a. The school buildings and associated facilities in the School Division shall be maintained in good repair and a high degree of cleanliness to ensure therein a comfortable and safe environment for students and School Board employees.

Section 6.2 – Maintenance and Planning Staff.

a. To achieve the goals stated in Section 6.1 above, the superintendent of schools shall recommend for employment persons deemed necessary to maintain existing facilities, to identify future needs, and to plan for the construction or renovation of facilities. (York Country Public Schools, 1992)

These policies state a desire on the part of the school system to keep the school facilities in good condition and also establish a work force charged with the responsibility of doing just that. These are the policies that establish some form of organization. Other policies are needed for specific tasks to be done. Some school systems have policies covering special programs, such as a renewal effort. School board policies from the Fairfax County(Va.) Public School system include the following:

Policy 7510.1 – DESIGN AND CONSTRUCTION
Building Modernization and Renewal

1. Evaluating Existing Buildings
   Existing older buildings shall be evaluated periodically to determine their ability to support the approved educational program and the safety and operability of the building systems.
2. Renewal Program
   A program for the renewal and updating of substandard older schools shall be an integral part of the Capital Improvement Program.

3. Scope of Renewal
   The same educational specifications shall be used in determining the scope of instructional facilities for renewals as are used for new schools. Structural, mechanical, and style specifications will follow the original design as much as feasible in order to minimize cost.
   Any major modernization shall extend the life cycle of buildings for 20 or more years. Buildings shall be selected for modernization based on the condition of the building, suitability of facilities to support the instructional program, and the long-range potential of the building.
4. Limited Renewal
   Where demographic studies indicate that a school may not be needed at its present location for more than five or ten years, consideration shall be given to limited renewal.
   In limited renewal, emphasis shall be placed on correcting operational and safety deficiencies. This may include correction of heating, ventilating, and plumbing problems, the replacement of ceiling or floor tiles, and elimination of all determinable safety hazards.
   Other minor renovations to the building and grounds which will improve the educational program may be accomplished during the limited renewal. In addition, painting, carpeting, and other aesthetic improvements to enhance the educational environment may also be accomplished during limited renewal. The determination of priorities within funding limits shall be accomplished in cooperation with the local school staff and community.

Building Evaluation and Renewal

1. Buildings shall be surveyed by the Department of Design and Construction with advice and assistance of instructional and support service personnel.
2. School principals shall submit reports of deficiencies within their buildings to the Department of Design and Construction through the area superintendent.
3. Existing older buildings shall be inspected and evaluated as needed to establish requirements for renewal under the Capital Improvement Program.
4. All new construction and renewals shall be inspected and evaluated nine months after completion to ascertain deficiencies requiring correction prior to expiration of warranty.
5. Buildings shall again be evaluated after seven years' use to determine adequacy and ability of building design and systems to properly support the educational program and function.
6. Renewal efforts shall be guided by the educational specifications to assure equivalency in scope and size of instructional program facilities which will permit the educational program to be carried out in full. In the application of these educational specification to renewals, two premises will be observed:
   a. Maximum utilization will be made of existing facilities. The design

of the basic systems (structural, electrical, plumbing, heating/ventilation, air conditioning) of the existing building will be preserved, and components will be replaced and/or upgraded as required but the systems will not be totally destroyed and replaced with different systems for the sake of making them more modern or to make an older physical plant look like a newer school.

b. The size of the facilities called for in the educational specification will be reduced only to adjust for differences in the program capacity of the building. The scope and size of facilities in a school to be renewed may be increased to utilize existing spaces and minimize the expense of remodeling or new construction. (Fairfax County Public Schools, 1977)

These school board policies relate specifically to the maintenance and renovation function of the school system. These policies give guidance to the department of school facilities on how the renewal program will work and the rules under which it will be administered, which gives assurance to the entire school organization that fairness and rationality will prevail in the renovation or renewal of all school buildings.

SCHOOL FACILITIES ORGANIZATION

The complexity of the organization and resultant number of employees is obviously determined by the size of the school system. In regards to the facilities department, the size of the staff and responsibility for certain functions is determined by the number of school buildings. In large schools, the school facilities department may well employ hundreds of people simply for the planning activities associated with constructing new facilities. In addition, the maintenance department may employ thousands of workers in many crafts. In a recent survey of schools in Virginia, the range of maintenance workers in each school system was from 0 to over 280 (Earthman, 1991). In the case where the school system did not have any maintenance workers, the city owned the buildings and provided all of the maintenance work for the schools; consequently, the schools reported no maintenance employees on their payroll. The school system with over 280 craftspersons had a population in excess of 136,000 students in over 180 school buildings.

For the most part, schools do not have a large number of maintenance workers because the average school system in the United States is not large. With approximately 15,500 school systems legally organized in the country, only 754, or approximately 5 percent of the total, have a population in excess of 9,999 students (*U.S. Census Report,* 1987).

Consequently, not many school systems have an extensive and diversified maintenance staff. In most of these cases, the maintenance crew does only the simple repair work on school buildings and does not engage in serious renovation or renewal projects. Such projects are usually tendered for public bid on the open market and completed by private contractors. The size of the maintenance staff and the school planning staff is simply a function of the number of buildings to care for and the number of new classrooms that will be needed in the future. Larger school systems are constantly adding buildings to the inventory because of the growth of the student population. Obviously, the more buildings there are, the more maintenance staff are needed to keep the buildings in a state of good repair. Small school systems can afford maintenance workers only to the extent of need, which in turn is driven by the number of school buildings in use.

There are formulae available for determining the number of custodians needed to keep a building clean (Castaldi, 1994); however, there is no formula to determine the number of maintenance workers needed. The decision regarding the size of the maintenance staff of the school system is primarily a political decision and secondarily a value decision. The desire to keep the buildings in excellent condition is shaped and molded by the community through the school board. The community decides who will be on the school board and, through these persons, decides how well the buildings will be kept. If the community values well-maintained buildings, the school board and administration will employ sufficient crew to do just that. Conversely, the desire to maintain a certain tax rate level may result in a small maintenance staff and undoubtedly a poorer condition of buildings. School administrators have a great deal of influence in formulating these policies. Oftentimes attention paid to well-maintained buildings by the superintendent of schools is enough to cause the community to want their buildings kept in excellent shape.

In large school systems, the functions of maintenance and operations are often included in the school facilities division of the school system. Under this broad umbrella, there are different departments responsible for different functions in planning for schools. Figure 3.1 on page 29 illustrates the line and staff chart for the school facilities division of a very large school system. Five separate departments are under the office of the Associate Superintendent for School Facilities: Land Acquisition, School Planning, Architecture and Construction, Supplies and Equipment, and Maintenance and Operations. The Architecture and Construction Department is further divided into sub-departments of Design and Construction.

In a school system as large as the one portrayed in Figure 3.1, there may be as many as 225 employees working in the planning process to provide safe and modern housing for the student population. Each department plays a different role, but all contribute to the completion of capital projects, be they a new high school or a light bulb replacement. The entire school facilities division is augmented by the Research and Evaluation Department and the Budget and Financial Planning Department. The Research and Evaluation Department provides the School Facilities Division with student enrollment projections and a demographic analysis of student population. The Budget and Financial Planning Department provides all of the financial support needed to obtain and expend funds. In an organization as large as this, the planning for a complete renovation project would be well within the capabilities of the in-house staff.

Maintenance projects needed by the school system may be done by the crew of the school system or tendered for bid to an outside contractor, depending upon the nature and magnitude of the project. The decision is made by the school administrators based upon several things, including availability of school system maintenance staff with the expertise needed to complete the project, complexity of the project, the dollar amount of the project, and the time for completion of the project. Even in a large school system the scope of the maintenance project that can be completed by school system staff is limited. In a renewal or renovation of an existing school building, the design and construction of the project is contracted to outside sources. The only part of the project that is completed by school system employees is soliciting bids.

These bids should include planning, for in small school systems, the facilities planning staff is usually not large enough to complete the necessary planning for a renovation or building renewal project. Additional planning expertise can range from educational consultants who can advise on the physical needs of the educational program, to architects who can provide design and engineering expertise. A big distinction must be made here in that the educators, whether they be employees of the school system or consultants to the school system, are the persons who can adequately interpret the physical needs of the educational program in terms of kinds and number of spaces. After that is done, the architects then decide how these needs can be met within the current physical envelope of the building.

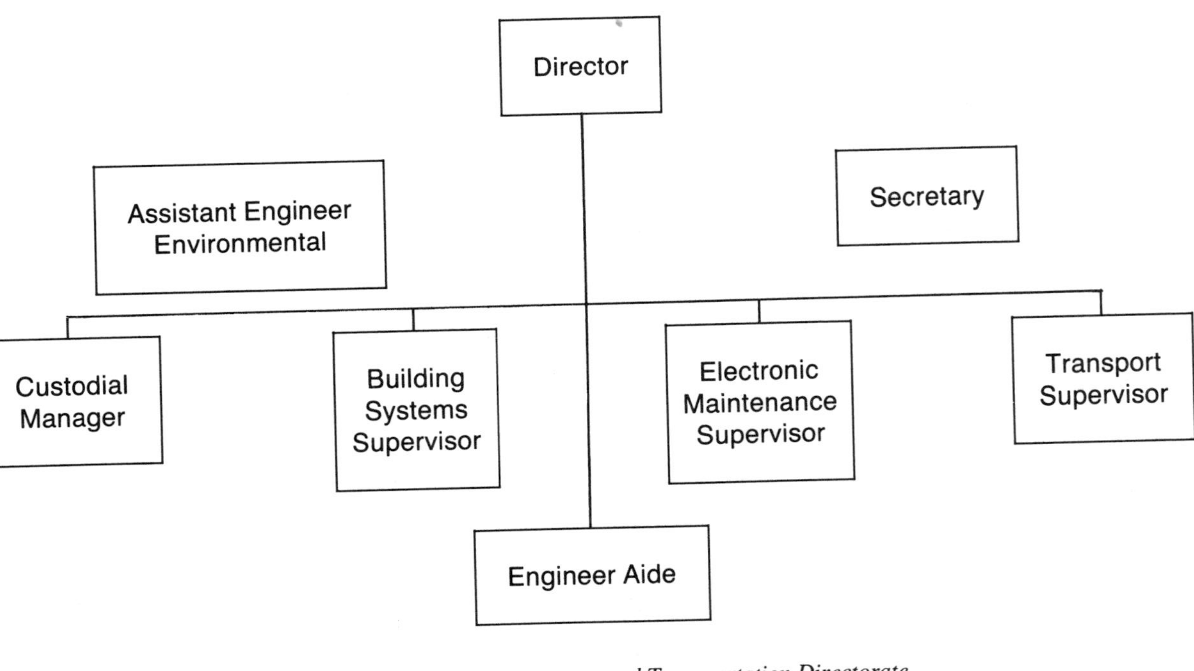

Figure 3.2. *Facility Maintenance and Transportation Directorate.*

Staffing of the department responsible for maintaining the existing buildings in a small school system is extremely important. The employees must be carefully selected to provide the needed expertise in planning for such work. Figure 3.2, above, illustrates the organization of the maintenance function within a small- to medium-sized school system of approximately 9,000 students or less.

As shown, the entire operation is headed by the Director of Maintenance and Transportation in contrast to a larger school system where an associate superintendent is in charge of school facilities operation. The majority of the planning expertise in the larger school systems is absent from this organizational chart because the need for planning many new buildings is not great; however, the persons in the various positions in small school systems have considerable planning responsibility over a wide range of problems. In other words, employees in small school systems must be responsible for the planning of more than one phase of maintenance and cannot specialize. Small school systems must rely considerably upon outside assistance for much of their renovation, renewal, and modernization programs.

REFERENCES

Castaldi, B. 1994. *Educational Facilities: Planning, Modernization, and Management. 4th Edition.* Boston: Allyn and Bacon, p. 435.

Earthman, G. I. 1991. *Survey of School Facility Expenditures in Virginia.* Blacksburg, VA: College of Education, Virginia Polytechnic Institute and State University, p. 187.

Fairfax County Public Schools. 1977. *School Board Regulations.* Fairfax, VA.

United States Census Bureau. 1987. *U.S. Census Report.*

York County Public Schools. 1992. Chapter 6, *School Board Policies.* Yorktown, VA.

CHAPTER 4

Planning within the Educational Organization

INTRODUCTION

PLANNING is the most extensive and pervading administrative activity of any organization. It is also the most important administrative activity performed within the framework of an organization. This is especially true of the many educational systems and organizations throughout the country. All employees of the school system engage in planning activities not only during the working day, but also during off-hours. Planning is also a consuming instructional activity for staff. Teachers plan at all times, including after school hours, to meet the needs of their students. They engage in short-term planning on almost a minute-by-minute basis for various lessons, use of material, or student needs; but they also plan for a year-long program, by establishing some annual goals for their students. Even the students themselves plan for various activities and goals. Likewise, principals engage in the same type and kinds of planning as do teachers and students. They meet immediate needs and problems through planning, yet they assist the staff in establishing annual goals and objectives. Further, principals and staff plan for certain goals and objectives that necessitate a term of activities beyond the stretch of even one year. The same can be said for departments and administrators in a central administrative office. Planning seems to be second nature to the members of the educational establishment no matter at which level of the organization they are located.

In spite of the fact that educators are experts in the planning process and daily engage in planning activities, sometimes the organizational planning process does not operate in a closely coordinated fashion. The school system is a very complicated and complex organization with many levels of responsibility and many isolated planning units. The complexity of the system works against a coordinated planning effort and can make such a planning effort extremely difficult. Lack of communication is probably the greatest deterrent to coordinated planning followed closely by the inability to identify where and how a particular activity relates to an overall organizational goal.

NATURE OF PLANNING

The planning requirements of a school system are much like they are in any other organization dealing with people. Planning is necessary so that an organization can succeed in its goals. There are many reasons for planning, but usually these reasons center around completing or achieving an objective. Planning becomes the central focus within any combined effort of formal organization to guide internal activities.

All public school systems are constantly plagued by limited resources, and as a result, educators must make the best use of whatever resources are available to them. This is so very true in today's world where there is severe competition between various local and state organizations for public resources. This situation makes it even more imperative that school systems plan for the prudent use of resources. There are other purposes for planning within the context of the school system, most of which deal with goals and resources. Suggested purposes for planning are:

- to identify acceptable goals
- to use properly the resources available to the successful pursuit of adopted goals
- to conserve limited resources
- to marshall staff cooperation and input into completion of goals (Earthman, 1986)

Only through effective planning can an organization identify goals that are eventually acceptable to all concerned persons. This is done through the process of developing a plan of action that incorporates significant goal identification procedures. Needs assessment activities, environmental scanning, and similar types of activities are essential methods used to identify goals. Even the activity of brainstorming can help educators identify goals. Crafting a vision and/or mission statement for the organization also helps in the process of goal identification.

Once the goals have been identified and approved, the staff must then actively work toward the goals by applying resources. The proper use of limited resources goes a long way in helping the school system effectively pursue organizational goals. Planning enables the school staff to identify the amount of resources necessary to accomplish the goals and how these resources can be utilized in an efficient manner.

Planning also enables the staff to constructively conserve the limited resources of the school system. School systems never have sufficient resources for the responsibilities the communities assign them and, as a result, staff members are constantly trying to discharge ever increasing responsibilities with increasingly diminished resources. Only by parsimonious use of resources through planning can the schools meet their goals.

Finally, administrators must encourage the staff to actively support the effort to meet goals. This can best be done by involving the staff in the planning process. One of the purposes for planning is involvement by the staff, so they will not only have a say in identifying and adopting the goals, but also in implementing the effort. Staff members will become aware of and approve of goals they have helped craft through their involvement in planning.

PLANNING RESPONSIBILITY

Planning is not something that is done by someone else for the school system. Planning is an integral part of the day-by-day activities of the people employed by the school system. Sometimes, though, it is rather difficult for persons, even within the school system, to properly visualize the planning effort of the organization. To many people, planning is something done by someone else that really has no effect on them. This is a rather parochial view of the organizational world, but nevertheless, one widely held by persons in school systems. Even though few people would actually admit to believing such a thing, their actions often reveal their belief that planning is external to their spheres of activity.

The superintendent of schools is responsible for the system-wide planning that takes place as well as for the quality of that planning. The superintendent can take credit for a well-functioning planning effort, but must also take the blame when the planning effort does not work well or when there has been no planning effort. The effectiveness of planning is directly related to the expertise of the superintendent and to the conception of planning held by that person. Planning simply does not happen without some effort on the part of the head of the organization;

consequently, it is the superintendent who must organize the staff to do the planning. This planning effort must embody several important concepts of planning. For instance, the superintendent must decide who will be involved in the planning process, provide working resources, and communicate the importance of this effort to the staff. The superintendent must set the scope of the planning effort by defining how broad the planning effort is and limiting the length of time allocated to the process. Likewise, even the direction of the effort is stipulated by the superintendent.

Planning can stem from the top down, that is, from the central office down to the individual schools, or the effort can be from the bottom up. Although there are probably no true extremes as far as the direction of planning is concerned, whether the process goes up or down should be indicated by the superintendent. There can never be a complete upward process for planning from the bottom to the top because of the structure of public school systems and the fact that the school board is charged by the community with the overall control and direction of the school system. All of the decisions regarding the nature, context, and method of planning must be made by the superintendent before a planning effort can seriously begin.

The most important decision the superintendent makes concerns the staffing of the effort, especially the designation of the person to head the process. If this planning is for the entire school system and entails a major long-range planning effort, a person or office should be designated as the responsible agency for actually doing the planning. In most school systems one person is designated as the planning officer. In small school systems, this person also has other responsibilities in addition to the planning process. That person may also be responsible for research and evaluation programs, testing programs, pupil personnel, instructional programs, or any number of activities. The smaller the school system, the more tasks and responsibilities are assigned to each person or office. In these situations the person in charge of planning must balance the planning activities with other demands of the office. Considerable planning effort must then be expended by other members of the school system to compensate for the lack of a formal planning staff.

In some small- or medium-sized schools the person responsible for planning is an administrative assistant located in the superintendent's office. In large school systems, there may well be a director of planning or someone with a similar designation. In extremely large school systems, there may be an assistant or associate superintendent for planning on the staff. Such offices are staffed with professionals who can assist those persons involved in the planning process. Planning offices that are staffed with planning experts are very common in large school systems.

THE PLANNING PROCESS

Planning is a continuous process in every school system and is done on several levels. The system-wide planning process is probably more formal than planning at the school building or departmental levels, but the same methodology of planning is used regardless of the level on which the planning is done. The basic methodology of planning consists of a process of problem-solving, which requires decision making. The various steps or stages in planning are usually thought of as the following:

(*1*) Identification of the problem or goal
(*2*) Identification of the data needed
(*3*) Formulation of alternative solutions
(*4*) Identification and selection of preferred solution
(*5*) Application or implementation of a process or a solution
(*6*) Evaluation of the results

These are the fundamental activities people engage in while planning. Each of these activities may be extremely complicated and use a great deal of data, or they may be very elementary because of the simplicity of the task and the small amount of data involved. The complexity of the planning process is determined by the goal or purpose and the amount of data used in the process. Obviously, it is simpler to plan a class field trip than to plan for a new school, yet each activity uses the same planning process. Most experts in the field of planning, however, seem to agree that this basic process is used in all types of planning regardless of what is planned, the length of planning time, or the amount of data involved.

Some planning experts seem to differentiate between lengths of planning time. For instance, Lewis (1983) mentions three types of planning that use the same basic methodology, yet differ in the length of time needed to complete them. Lewis lists these types of planning as (1) problem solving, (2) operational, and (3) strategic. Problem-solving deals with problems or events of short durations; perhaps the maximum time would be three months. Operational planning refers to planning for a year in advance and is usually tied into the operational budgeting process of the school system. Strategic planning refers to those activities that deal with problems, projects, and activities that consume three to seven years. Most school systems use strategic planning activities to develop long-range plans.

Some authors in the field of planning differentiate between strategic and long-range planning (Kaufman, 1988). Strategic planning is more fluid, uses more sophisticated data, scans the environment of the school, and identifies a general direction in which the school system should move. Strategic planning identifies goals for the school system which are in keeping with the environmental needs of the community. Long-range planning is linear; its based upon limited data that do not address the immediate environment of the school system and are not inclusive. The debate between strategic and long-range planning is probably more a matter of interpretation than of substance. Both planning models incorporate a comprehensive approach to planning for the future and use basically the same methodology. Strategic planning uses an environmental scanning that can easily be used in long-range planning. In other words, the difference in the planning models is in terminology, not in methodology. Strategic planning is planning for the long term; however, long-range planning may or may not incorporate some of the data inputs that strategic planning does, but the possibility for those inputs does exist. Strategic planning seems to be the current term to explain the system-wide comprehensive planning effort that so many school systems employ. Each model, however, produces a planning document which can be called a long-range or strategic plan.

PLANNING PRODUCT

The end result of any planning process is some type of planning document. This document could be a product that is used by teachers in the school system, such as a curriculum guide, or it could be a manual for personnel procedures. It could also be a proposed budget either for the school system, a school building, or a department within the school system. Finally, the document could be a plan itself. This most often is the case when a long-range plan is prepared for adoption by the school board.

LONG RANGE PLAN

The long-range plan will assist the school board and staff in determining the direction, measuring the efforts, and applying the resources of the school system. The long-range plan should provide data on all aspects of school system operation, especially those parts of the organization where the action must take place and the parts of the surrounding environment that affect the school. The following elements or segments are usually discussed and included in a long-range plan for the school system:

(*1*) Community resources (environmental scanning)
   - population demographics, physical features, socio-economic description, social services, parks/recreation, museums, and other resources the schools can use
   - Forces that impact upon the school system, conditions in the community to which the school must address efforts

(*2*) The educational program
   - vision statement
   - mission statement
   - goal, objectives, behavioral objectives
   - subject content distribution by grades
   - teaching strategies
   - new program initiatives
   - present and needed staff configuration

(*3*) Clientele to be served
   - projection of student population for five to ten years
   - description of where students live
   - description of types/kinds of students

(*4*) Facilities available and needed
   - description of available facilities and improvements needed
   - description of new facilities needed

(*5*) Financial plan
   - operational funds program and budget
   - capital funds plans and budget

In the situation where the product of a planning effort is a specific plan, such as a long-range plan, the resultant document is used as a guide by the staff in discharging program responsibilities. In other words, the staff—central office, administrative, and teaching—use a long-range plan as a guide for further planning and action. In addition, the staff has to develop other work plans or plans of action to deal with the large, overall, system-wide plan in a meaningful way. The long-range plan is not something to be placed on the shelf and forgotten once it has been approved by the school board.

A long-range plan can be a massive document and is not really meant to be implemented so much as give direction to every member of the school system. Various segments of the long-range plan are sifted out and used as a basis for the development of action or work plans. In other words, the action/work plans are derived and formulated to address what needs to be accomplished in each part of the overall school system's long-range plan. For instance, the long-range plan should describe what new educational initiatives will be implemented within the planning period; however, describing the initiatives alone is not enough. An action plan must be developed to insure that the initiatives are implemented. In this case, the director of curriculum, the assistant superintendent for instruction, or the office responsible for this phase of the school system must develop such a work or action plan. Only through this process will the educational initiatives be in place at the appropriate time and location. Likewise, the new educational initiatives might require additional staff with certain capabilities. If so, additional teachers and support personnel must be identified, employed, and trained so that the staff will be in place for the beginning of these new educational programs. Thus, the director of personnel or someone in a similar position must develop a plan of action or work schedule to do just that. Such a document might be termed the human resource plan for the school system. In this plan, the personnel office details what actions need to be taken to insure the correct number of staff members with the capabilities needed are at the right place at the right time.

There are other segments of the long-range plan that need to be addressed by action/work plans:

- curriculum development plan—developed by the director of curriculum and instruction
- instructional development plan—developed by the director of instruction/secondary/elementary
- human resource plan—developed by the director of personnel
- staff development plan—developed by the director of staff development
- capital improvement plan—developed by the director of facilities

- financial plan: operational and capital–developed by the director of budget or business manager

All of these action plans are important and absolutely necessary for the successful operation of the school system. The only way a long-range plan will be implemented is to follow an action plan.

PLANNING RENOVATIONS AND MAINTENANCE

Where, then, does the maintenance and renovation of buildings fit into the overall planning scheme of the school system? Many school systems have a systematic preventative maintenance program and/or a regular schedule for the renovation of buildings, and a master plan or schedule for their completion. This schedule can be independent of the strategic planning effort of the school system because the various items included in the preventative maintenance program must be done during a certain year regardless of the type of educational program in operation in the school. In addition, a regularly scheduled renovation program could be determined by the age of the building independent of other planning efforts.

There are, however, some considerations about both the maintenance and renovation programs that impinge upon the strategic and operational planning efforts of the school system. One important consideration is related to funding. This is especially true for the maintenance program which is funded through the operational budget of the school. The proper funding of the maintenance program is always a concern in planning for the operational budget. The cost of the maintenance program for the year must be factored early into the budget. This means the cost of each item in the overall package must be determined early in the school year and included in the first draft of the budget. Depending upon the budgetary calendar, the input should be ready by at least October of the year preceding the budget's formal approval.

The strategic plan or long-range plan can also impact the maintenance program, in that certain improvement items in a building may need to be included to accommodate a new or expanded educational program. These items result from an evaluation of a school building to determine its ability to accommodate certain programs and activities. The strategic planning effort will at some time or other identify new educational initiatives that the school system wishes to implement. These educational initiatives could well demand a change in the structure of the school building. Perhaps new or different types of spaces will be needed for a new educational program. Changes in the internal structure of the school building may be needed to accommodate a certain activity that is part of the new educational program. In this manner, the strategic planning effort and the resultant long-range plan will impact the renovation program. Physical changes in the building, demanded by the new programs and contained in the long-range plan, will have to be included in the renovation project for the schools, both during the current year and subsequent years. In developing the educational specifications for the renovation project, the maintenance department will have to confer with the instructional department to insure that whatever physical features are needed will be included. In this manner the strategic planning effort of the school system is completed.

REFERENCES

Earthman, G. 1986. *Administering the Planning Process for Educational Facilities.* Jerico, NY: Wilkerson Publishers.

Kaufman, R. 1988. *Planning Educational Systems.* Lancaster, PA: Technomic Publishing Co.

Lewis, J., Jr. 1983. *Long-Range and Short-Range Planning for Educational Administrators.* Newton, MA: Allyn and Bacon, Inc.

CHAPTER 5

Financing the Renovation Project

INTRODUCTION

THE secret of success in planning for capital construction projects, as in most other ventures, is to plan in such a manner that funds will be available to implement the plan when needed. The implementation of a plan for a new school building or the renovation of an existing building needs appropriate funds at a propitious time to complete the proposed project. Without such planning, activities preceding the funding are a waste of the school system's resources. No school system staff enters into a planning effort, no matter what the subject or project, with no prospect of funding the operation. Part of the planning effort is seeking funds. In the case of renovations, such funding is necessary at the time of decision, or the beginning of the project.

SCHOOL FUNDING

There are many sources of revenue available to the local school system, including grants, gifts, loans, and taxes. School systems receive funds from the federal, state, and local governments; from a host of private sources such as foundations, booster clubs, and individual gifts; and from rental operations – the amount of these funds is extremely small compared to the total school budget, but rental fees do contribute to the revenues of a school system; and from student fees, also part of the revenues of the school system, again, these fees are so small they hardly cover the cost of the textbooks and materials used by a student during the year. Funds from all of these sources can be used to provide an educational program for the students. These funds are usually channelled into the local operational budget and expended from it. The manner in which these funds are obtained and the sources of the funds greatly govern how they can be used. Nevertheless, school systems plan their operational budget based upon the funds received from these sources.

Gifts to school systems, no matter what the source, can be accepted and used for whatever purpose the school board desires, unless there is some restrictive codicil to which the school board agrees. In some rare instances, funding sources outside the school system provide revenues for the construction of new school buildings. One example was the Impacted Aid Program of the Landrum Act of 1941, which did provide federal funds for the construction of schools that were needed because of the impact of armed services personnel moving into local school systems (Earthman, 1992). Another piece of federal legislation, the Emergency Relief Act of 1983, provided construction funds for localities to rebuild schools and other governmental buildings destroyed by floods. These two acts have been terminated and federal funds for any type of construction or rebuilding are no longer available under either measure. Almost without exception, however, sources identified above did not provide funds directly for renovation of existing schools. Although there may be some federal funds that can be used for improvement of vocational education facilities, federal funding for renovations, renewals, or modernization of regular educational facilities is virtually non-existent.

State Funding

States discharge their responsibility for educating children by assisting local school systems with operational funds for specified programs. These funds are usually distributed through some sort of grant-in-aid program. There are two ways state funds can be given to localities, namely, through grants and loans. Grants from states to local school systems usually fall into one of the following three types of grants: equalization, flat, and matching. Within these three types of grants, states can also make grants for funding capital construction projects or for paying debt service. Funds from a construction grant can be used to reimburse the local school system directly for a projects costs upon completion. Grants for debt service are funds that can be used to reduce the annual debt payment of a school system after local funds have been used to actually construct the building. In this type of grant, the local school system must actually go into debt through the bonding process to obtain the funds to complete the project and then apply for funds to help defray the cost of debt payments.

Flat grants, no matter what the purpose, are funds distributed on the basis of the number of pupils, teachers, classroom units, total population, or even on the number of buildings owned and operated by a local school system. These grants provide the school system with a set amount of money for each pupil, teacher, classroom, or some other designation. Some states provide a flat grant of a certain amount of money for each student enrolled in the school. In the case of those states which provide flat grants for construction purposes, these funds can be used for either new construction or renovations. The State of Mississippi has a capital support program which distributes a set amount of money for each student enrolled and an advance of up to 75 percent of the estimated amount that will accrue within 20 years from the date the advance is authorized (Salmon et al., 1988). In 1988, the amount of funds authorized to be distributed in that state was eighteen dollars per pupil in Average Daily Attendance (ADA). Programs like these do not provide adequate funds for any but the most marginal capital construction projects.

Equalization grants, whether for capital construction or operational purposes, are given based upon some formula to provide relief to school systems with limited ability to pay, and yet to provide some funds to every school system in the state. The grant is sometimes based upon the relationship of the wealth of a locality to the wealth of the state, or some other measure of relationship. Wealth can be determined in a number of ways, usually by assessed valuation of property, income of residents, taxes paid, or some combination of the three. In funding educational programs, the number of students is also factored into the formula. School systems which do not have much wealth are favored in the distribution of available funds to help compensate for their inability to raise enough funds to cover a defined basic educational program. The ability of a local school system to pay for educational programs and buildings is usually tied to the determined wealth of the locality. In an equalized grant program for capital construction, the same method of determining local school system need as is used in basic educational support programs is used to distribute funds. In poorer school systems, a large share of a capital project is funded by the state, whereas the wealthier school systems are reimbursed with a small sum of the project's total costs.

In several states, a pre-determined, per-pupil construction cost is used to assist in the distribution. For instance, New York and Pennsylvania both use a dollar amount for a per-rated pupil capacity of a building to determine the amount of the state's contribution to the total project. The pre-determined dollar amount is multiplied by the student capacity of the building; and then multiplied by an equalization factor to determine how much the state will pay for a project.

The theory behind the equalization grant is to provide, as much as possible, a level playing field for all school systems in the state seeking funds to provide safe, modern school facilities. Equalization grants seek to establish a partnership between the state and the local school system whereby both contribute to funding school house improvements. Approximately sixteen states use an equalization grant program to assist local school systems with capital construction projects; six of these states also provide an equalization grant program for debt service payments (Salmon et al., 1988).

A matching grant program is much like its name implies; both the state and locality share in the burden of providing funds for school buildings. The State of Delaware is credited with being the only state to have a matching grants program to assist school systems in funding capital projects (Salmon et al., 1988). Also, Delaware pays 60 percent of the debt service for approved construction for all school systems. The local school pays the remaining 40 percent. In most states that use an equalized grant program, the local school system must contribute some of the cost of the project. This local effort can be in the form of a certain tax rate that has to be applied to the assessed valuation of property, or, possibly, in the form of a pre-determined amount of money.

In New Mexico, each locality must levy a pre-determined tax rate on all property in the school system in order to qualify for the state's contribution of funds. In this respect, the grant is a matching grant. The difference between a matching and equalization grant would be the factor used in determining the local contribution. If that factor is based upon some relationship between local wealth, no matter how determined, and the state wealth, there is a property of equalization in the program. Matching grants, on the other hand, simply mandate the state to contribute a certain percentage of the total cost regardless of the local school system's ability to pay for the project.

The following table illustrates the number of states that have various kinds of grant programs:

Number of States and Type of Program

Type of Grant	Type of Program	
	Capital Outlay	Debt Service
Equalization	16	6
Flat	4	4
Matching	1	1

Another method by which the state can assist the local school system with construction or renovation costs is through what is commonly termed construction loan programs. Construction loan programs are simply provisions whereby the local school system can borrow sufficient funds to complete a capital construction project from the state. The amount of the loan is paid back to the state over a stipulated period of time. Two features of the construction loan program that are noteworthy are the provision for low interest rates and the extended pay-back period. Both these features make the loan program a viable option for the school system. The major drawback is that usually the funds available through this program are extremely limited. Most states have some form of restriction on the amount of funds a school system can borrow from the fund for each project. Thus, the ease with which a school system can borrow is tempered by the lack of sufficient funds to cover the needed projects. Only seven states have provisions for capital loans to local school systems.

Full state funding of capital construction projects is limited to three states: Alaska, California, and Hawaii. These states supply the funds for all construction of new schools and the major renovations and additions to existing schools. Hawaii has only one local school system and, as a result, the state provides full funding for all aspects of the educational enterprise on the islands. In fact, the local school systems cannot legally levy taxes of any form. In contrast, California stipulates full funding of capital construction projects, yet local school systems do have the ability to raise funds for renovations, renewals, or modernization of existing buildings.

Although the school system organization is indigenous to the geography of the state, Alaska does provide for the major share of capital construction funds. The provisions, however, call for the state to make 80 percent of the payments for the retirement of principal and interest on school construction bonds. The balance of the costs are borne by the local school systems. In essence, the only state where local funds do not pay for school buildings would be Hawaii and that is because of the uniqueness of the local governmental organization. All states do, however, contribute in an indirect manner to the maintenance of local school buildings through their contributions to the operational budgets of the schools. In 1981, the state legislature of Maryland passed a measure requiring the state to provide full funding of all major construction of school buildings. Undergirding this law was the attempt to equalize the quality of school facilities throughout the state and relieve local school systems of the burden of paying for school buildings. The law was administered by the Interagency Committee for Public School Construction under the Board of Public Works of Maryland. Under this program, major renovations, renewals, or modernization of existing buildings were included along with new construction. The original legislation was designed for full funding; however, the heavy burden of full funding of all capital construction projects in the state, plus the down-turn in the state's economy, caused a modification of the program. The bond funds and legislative appropriations do not now meet the total cost of providing adequate school buildings throughout the state. Maryland currently funds about 65 percent of the major construction projects presented to the Interagency Committee.

Building Authorities

Building authorities are quasi-governmental corporations, incorporated under the laws of the state, designed to assist state and local governmental units in obtaining suitable school housing for certain functions, such as educational programs. These authorities have also been used to enable school systems to obtain funds not ordinarily available, by circumventing restrictive debt limitations or bonding capabilities. In many states the debt ceiling or the assessed valuation of real property is so low that school systems cannot raise sufficient funds to construct proper buildings even if the property is taxed to the maximum. Both local and state governmental units have created building authorities to get around these restrictions. At the present time seven states have building authorities in existence. In five states there are local school building authorities and four state-level school building authorities are in operation. Both Kentucky and Pennsylvania have state and local school building authorities. Alaska, Maine, New Hampshire,

North Dakota, and Vermont use a bond bank, which is similar to the type of building authority that raises funds for local school systems (Salmon et al., 1988).

Building authorities can either raise funds to enable the school system to finance the construction of school buildings or construct the building themselves. In either method, the building authority raises funds through the sale of general obligation bonds and, as the case may be, either distributes the funds or constructs the building with the funds that were raised. The Virginia Public School Building Authority is an example of an authority on the state level that raises funds for local school systems.

The benefit of this procedure is that small school systems cannot obtain as low an interest rate on their own bonds as the building authority can. In addition, by combining the needs of many school systems, the building authority can tender for bid a sizable bond offer and attract more investors. All of the work entailed in marketing a bond issue is left to the building authority; the local school system does not stand the costs associated with selling bonds and administering the program. In addition, low interest rates and favorable repayment terms are available to the school system.

Authorities that actually construct facilities for local school systems are usually found in larger cities where the school system is fiscally dependent upon the local government. An example of this is the Chicago Public Building Authority, which is chartered by the city government and has the authority and capability to plan, employ an architect, monitor the design process, and supervise the construction of a school building. Even the major renovations, renewals, and modernizations of existing buildings are performed by this authority.

Local Funding

Funding of renovation, renewal, and modernization of existing building projects can be accomplished under either the operational or capital improvement budgets of the school system. Both of these methods of funding are used to some extent by all school systems. The size of the project to be completed, the capability of the maintenance crew, and the availability of revenue in the budget oftentimes determine the method of funding. For the most part, the major share of the maintenance program is funded through the operational budget, which in turn is financed through various tax sources.

Within the operational budget of every school system in the country is a section devoted to maintenance and operations functions. The maintenance and operations function is a major portion of that budget, oftentimes equalling 4–6 percent of the total budget amount. This budget section is usually divided into (1) the maintenance of the school plant and grounds, and (2) the operations of the plant. Contained under the operations section are all of the costs of cleaning and operating the schools. Costs include salaries for all employees, utility charges, operation of the motor vehicles, and supplies. The maintenance section of the budget includes the following categories of expenses:

- maintenance employees salaries and benefits
- repair/replacement of equipment
- repair/replacement of motor vehicles
- contracted maintenance
- equipment and maintenance contracted
- building materials
- contingencies

These categories also include the wages and salaries for all persons engaged in maintenance activities. Maintenance employees can be in clerical or supervisory positions, or workers in the crafts or trades. In addition, there is a large section of funds reserved for contracted maintenance projects. These are the projects which are considered too large or complicated for the school maintenance staff to complete and are tendered for public bid and completed by an outside contractor. This category contains the bulk of the funds allocated to maintenance activities. Also included in this section of the budget are funds to purchase building materials for the maintenance crew to use in repairing and maintaining school buildings.

General Obligation Bonds

In addition to the funds discussed above, school systems can go into debt to make some large purchases such as building a new school, buying new buses, or acquiring land. Most school systems cannot afford these purchases through annual operational funds, and find it necessary to obtain funds through other means. School systems fund capital projects by going into debt through the issuance of bonds. These bonds are called general obligation bonds or municipal bonds. These are debt instruments issued by any and all local governmental units, including school systems.

The bonds are a formal obligation which specifies in writing the conditions of repayment of the loan. They are legal instruments which pledge the full faith and credit of the school system towards repayment. Authority for issuing these types of bonds is usually obtained through a bond referendum of the people living in the school system. The bonds can be used for any purpose associated with capital improvements. They are most commonly used to plan and construct new buildings and additions and renovations to existing buildings.

The procedure for conducting a referendum is quite straightforward; however, there are considerable legal restrictions that must be met to successfully conduct the referendum. There is great similarity between the states as to the procedure, but the legal requirements do vary from state to state and are mandated by the state's constitution or statutes. Restrictions usually involve limitations on indebtedness, who is permitted to vote, votes needed for approval, types of bonds that can be issued, method of payment, limitations on tax rates, wording of the ballot, time limits for election notices, who can conduct an election, and voting procedures.

When the school board has decided to hold an election, a formal resolution to that effect must be made, approved by a majority of the members, and reflected in the official minutes of the meeting. This is the official notification that either the school system or other legal governmental unit will conduct the referendum. In many states, where the school system is separate from the local government and is a legal entity of the state, the school board can actually conduct the election. In such a situation, the school board either requests the superintendent to organize the election or appoints a board of tellers.

In most cases, the superintendent actually organizes the election, secures the personnel, produces the voting schedule, and presents this plan to the school board for its approval. If a board of tellers is appointed, the school board must still approve the procedure before the election can take place. In some situations, the board of tellers can be composed of persons from outside or inside the school system. In some jurisdictions the county or city board of elections, which is usually part of the local government, conducts the election for the school board. This is a much easier arrangement because the board of election has jurisdiction over the legal voter lists. If a school system conducts the election, the school board must obtain a copy of the official voter roll of the county or city to determine the voters. In some states the election is supervised by the circuit or other local court. In these instances, the court directs the local board of election to conduct the procedures for holding an election. In all cases, the legal restrictions of the state must be observed.

For the actual election, a ballot is prepared which simply states the proposition of going into debt for the purposes stated. In this situation the ballot would state something similar to "Do you favor going into debt in the amount of $_____ for the purposes of renovating, renewing, or modernizing the following existing school buildings?" A simple "yes" or "no" voter response is required. In some cases, a simple plurality is required for passage; in other cases 50 percent plus one vote is needed, and in other cases a higher percentage, such as 60, 66, or 75 percent, is required for approval. The results of the balloting is announced to the community, the court, the board of assessors, and the city or county treasurer. Following this, the board of elections officially announces the results of the election, notifies the board of assessors to levy the appropriate tax, and the treasurer is notified to collect the additional taxes.

Subsequently, the school board must prepare, print, and sell the bonds called for in the election. This process is extremely complicated and is carried out with the assistance of bond counsel and municipal bond selling companies. The funds collected by the treasurer for the purposes stipulated on the bond issue are then deposited in the appropriate bank for use by the school board. A capital improvement program is funded in this manner and the appropriate amount of funds are allocated to the various projects listed in that document. This, in very simplified form, stipulates how school systems obtain bond funds to carry out major renovations, renewals, and modernization of existing buildings.

REFERENCE

Salmon, R., C. Dawson, S. B. Lawton and T. L. Johns. 1988. *Public School Finance Programs of the United States and Canada: 1986–87.* Reston, VA: American Educational Finance Association & Virginia Polytechnic Institute and State University, p. 464.

CHAPTER 6

Developing the Program for Renovations

INTRODUCTION

THE two motivating factors in the decision to renovate a school building are change in educational program and age of the structure. Significant changes in the educational program are a sufficient justification to spend funds to renovate or renew an existing building. A school building becomes educationally obsolete long before it becomes structurally or mechanically obsolete. When a building does reach an age when it must be brought up-to-date structurally and mechanically, then the educational program must also be considered. Whenever any major renovation, renewal, or modernization takes place in a school building, consideration most be given to how the building will support the educational program in the future. To do otherwise is to make a grave administrative mistake.

The educational program should be the basis for and the driving force behind any changes in a building. The story is told of the school system that did a complete renovation of a 1930's structure that housed a junior high population. All major utility systems were improved or changed to bring them up-to-date. Even the structural system was improved – windows were replaced, a new roof was put into place, and carpeting was laid in the classrooms and hallways. The physical environment of the building was measurably improved. The space and interior of the school library, however, had never been changed since the building had opened, thirty-three years earlier. The renovation project, did not call for any improvements to that space. The result of the renovation project was that the structure was very much improved and its life extended. Unfortunately, the students and teachers were forced to continue using a library space that was designed over sixty years ago. Such lack of consideration for the educational program in a renovation project is totally inexcusable. If the renovation project adds years and even decades to the useful life of the structure, then the structure ought to be able to accommodate a modern educational program, no matter how it is defined.

Whether the initial motivation in a renovation project is to change the building to accommodate an educational program or because the age of the building requires it, the prime consideration should be to upgrade the building so it can support the most modern educational program possible, however that is defined. Based upon that premise, every major or complete renovation should first of all make provision for the educational program to be properly housed.

Some school systems have in place a school building renewal program designed to systematically update each older building to the standard of the most recently constructed building. Each year a certain number of buildings are slated to be renewed because they have reached a pre-determined age. Under this program, when a building is designated for renewal, all of the systems within the structure are brought up to a standard that is comparable to the newest school building in the school system. These systems could include electrical, plumbing, heating/ventilation/air conditioning, windows, roofs, and floor coverings. In addition, the structural shell is most often included in the evaluation for possible strengthening or improvement of the building. In these projects attention is always given to the provision for a barrier fee environment. At the same time, however, provisions are made for accommodating the educational program in the renovated space.

DEVELOPMENT OF EDUCATIONAL PROGRAM SPECIFICATIONS

There are basically two considerations when discussing the implications of a renovation project. These considerations are how the educational program can be accommodated in the existing building and how the physical envelope and systems of the building can be improved. These two considerations go hand-in-hand in developing the renovation plan.

When a building is scheduled for renovation, the educators in the school system have a chance to provide the spaces and equipment needed to properly implement programs that are either currently operating in the rest of the school system or not yet in existence. The renovation should include more than simply replacing the old equipment with new equipment, such as in the science laboratories or vocational education shops. In these situations, educators should ask how each subject is presently taught and how it will be taught in the future so that the space can accommodate the advances in teaching methodology. This question is particularly important in science programs. New equipment can be placed in the laboratory, but perhaps the methodology has changed so much that new configurations are needed. Replacing equipment is one thing; placing new equipment in a different configuration is quite another. The latter requires an educator knowledgeable in science subject matter and methodology, who can describe what is needed in a modern science laboratory. This is a rare opportunity that needs to be exploited as fully as possible if an older building is to be changed to accommodate a modern educational program.

Some of the changes that need to be made in the existing building may be stipulated by some general agreement or adopted policy of the school board. In other words, a renovation or renewal project automatically includes improvement to certain systems of the building. Other changes are the result of evaluations of the building. These evaluations seek to rectify current program demands for space and equipment in a building constructed with different program demands.

Most of the buildings being considered now and in the next decade for renovation were constructed in the 1950s. Many of these buildings were planned and designed for a traditional academic program. Classrooms and laboratories, for example, were grouped around the various subjects taught in school. These buildings were characterized by departmental groupings of classrooms such as English, history, mathematics, science, music, and vocational education. The problem then becomes one of changing an existing structure, built under different program assumptions, to conform to new and different program demands. These decisions must be made by either trained educators within the school system or educational consultants employed from the outside. The result is a document called "educational specifications." The effort entails identification of need or program and then translating this into space requirements. The analysis demands a great deal of considered professional experience and knowledge regarding educational program practice and state requirements for space.

The end product of the analysis is a printed document which is generally termed educational specifications and is used by architects to design the renovated building. After defining the educational program that will be conducted in the building, detailed down to individual courses to be offered, the next step is relating these program demands to specific planning requirements such as space, equipment, and relationships. The process and result of the analysis is then reported by narrative description, graphic presentation, equipment identification, and pictorial display.

The document contains a specific explanation of the educational program in terms of two processes that occur in the school. These are the processes teachers use in teaching a specific subject or activity and the processes students use to learn what is being taught. These two processes occur simultaneously in the classroom and must be accounted for in allocating space. To present data on these processes, the educator must ask these questions: "What kinds of activities does a teacher engage in to effectively teach this subject matter, skill, or attitude?" and, "What kinds of activity does a student engage in to effectively learn what is being taught?"

The answer to these questions will be the basis for describing the environment in which these processes will take place and the equipment needed. This description will spell out in specific terms the amount of space needed for certain activities, the kinds of equipment and material needed for support, and where this space should be located.

The task in programming a renovation project is not much different from programming for a new school building. The same questions need to be asked in both situations. The difference, however, is that there are given spaces in which subject areas are presently located in the building. If the subject area is moved, where will it be located? The existing walls sometimes become a barrier to making some changes in location for a subject area. Oftentimes the configuration of a building prescribes the amount of change in location that can be accomplished. For example, one current organizational change that is popular is the idea of grouping students in one area of the building in what is commonly termed a house. Instruction in several subjects are offered to the students in the house so that they can stay in one area of the school building for a number of periods of study. This obviously eliminates some of the student movement throughout the building. At the same time this grouping pattern allows teachers to cooperatively plan the instructional program for a certain group of students. This organizational plan needs to have a number of classrooms located contiguously in one area of the building in order to be successful. In most older buildings, classrooms are stretched out along a corridor which serves as the major circulation area.

Obviously, with this kind of traffic and a linear configuration of classrooms, it is difficult to establish a sense of a house organization and a feeling on the part of the students of being together as a group. Only by severe demolition could a satisfactory house plan be possible in some older school buildings.

Nevertheless, the task of the educational programmer is to seek ways to implement a given program in a building designed for a different program. As stated above, the first step is to recognize and order the educational program and to describe it in detail. Following this, these activities can be supported by specific space planning requirements and eventually related to other requirements and needed equipment.

Programming Responsibility

The responsibility for programming a renovation project rests solely with the school system. The decisions that need to be made regarding educational programs are such that only educators can intelligently make them. The school staff is the legal representative of the school board and by reason of that position, must make certain recommendations regarding program implementation. Sometimes making these decisions and recommendations is very difficult because there are competing demands by various segments of the community and educational establishment. Nonetheless, only the educational staff can make these recommendations to the school board, and only after careful study. The absence of a decision is no reason for the decision to be made by the architect. Sometimes educators hesitate to make a decision and thereby create a leadership vacuum. When a leadership vacuum occurs, someone always steps in to make a decision. In cases of renovations, sometimes architects will step in to make a decision so they can proceed with their work because they are under a schedule to complete the project. This is a case of the educational establishment and school board abrogating their responsibility.

One person in the school system should be charged with the responsibility for guiding the planning activities used to develop the educational specifications. This person should be charged with the responsibility of gathering sufficient data from appropriate personnel and groups to actually write a program specification document. This responsibility consumes considerable time and should not be assigned to a person already engaged in a full-time position. This responsibility is too important to be delegated, and should not be an added task for someone to complete whenever time permits.

The person responsible for preparing the set of educational specifications needs support and resources to complete the task. These resources include staff to plan meetings, gather data, write minutes and reviews of meetings, report production, and develop files of information. The person responsible for this task should have access to the facilities of the local school. So long as this is the primary task, one person can easily handle all of the responsibilities associated with this phase of the planning process. That person should have some competence in group processes and consensus building in order to work effectively with the people involved in the project. Sometimes teachers or administrators can be released from their positions for a time to head up this effort. The length of time might be as much as three months, but the small amount of funds expended for that period of time is more than compensated for by a better school.

Planning Involvement

A major part of developing a set of educational specifications for the renovation of a building is involving people. The person guiding this process should have some competence in group processes and consensus-building activities. That person must also be aware of the various groups and individuals that should be involved in data gathering and decision making for the project. In many school systems, there is a set protocol for deciding who is to be involved and how. Protocols are developed to give guidance to the person in charge so that various groups are not excluded from the process.

There are three major groups of individuals that should be involved in developing the educational specifications: the local school staff, parents and community members, and the central staff as represented by supervisors and directors of subject areas. Not all of the groups are involved in the same way. For instance, the local teachers need to be involved because they are the ones who will actually be teaching in the renovated school. This group may not, however, actually determine the extent of the curriculum to be offered in the newly renovated school. This decision may well belong to members of the central administrative staff and the office of the superintendent. The local teaching staff can best reflect the needs of the students in that part of the school system.

For this reason alone, they need to be significantly involved. This involvement may also permit the teachers to grow through being challenged with new ideas from the outside. If an educational consultant is employed to develop educational specifications, that person should bring some new ideas into the process for consideration. In a renovation or renewal project, just like a new school building, the teaching staff should strive toward improving the instructional program by participating in the planning process, because they will be teaching in improved facilities. In other words, the planning for a renovation project should be a form of staff development for the local school staff because they will deal with possible changes in curricular materials and methodology.

Another group that will be involved in a renovation project will be the central office staff. In medium to large school systems, this staff may be rather large, but each subject area should be included in the process. These individuals should be the most versed people in the school system for new ideas in their field. They should be on the cutting edge of the discipline as far as new educational methodologies are concerned. They will be instrumental in suggesting methods of teaching and changes in curricular content. These people should be involved in a series of exchanges on a group-by-group or discipline-by-discipline basis. The parameters of the size of the project should be explained and their role in the process defined. The suggestions of these groups and individuals should then be reviewed by the local teaching staff before being incorporated into the educational specifications. Planning the curriculum and instructional methodology even for a renovated existing building is a sizable job that requires consideration of future needs. The educational planning for all construction projects, even a renovation project, needs to begin long before the time needed for educational specification development. If changes or improvements in the educational program are going to occur in conjunction with a renovation project, many decisions have to be made early. Sufficient time is needed before beginning the renovation project to make these decisions and to arrive at consensus.

The third group that needs significant involvement in the planning process is the local community, which is composed of many groups and individuals. The big question is "Who should be involved and to what extent?" Each school system must decide the answer to this question and many have a school board policy delineating the precise manner in which the community will be involved in such projects. In the absence of any directive for involvement, the educational planner should provide a forum for the community to express its wishes and to understand the project.

There are several reasons for involving the community in the planning process. First of all, a renovation of an existing building is an important aspect of community life. Renovating a school building tells the community the school system believes in its existence and supports its growth. Secondly, a renovation project is good advertisement for the school system in the local community. By involving people the school system is, in effect, letting the community have a say in what happens in what the community believes is its own school. Lastly, involvement will insure that the community will buy into the project and support it. In this respect, if the school system needs to hold a bond election, the community will be more apt to support it.

Review and Approvals

The person in charge of the development of educational specifications will need to provide feedback and secure approvals as the work progresses. The feedback should be in the form of a review of the work done in previous planning sessions. Decisions agreed upon previously need to be emphasized and new material reviewed for additional decisions. This systematic review is the only way to gain consensus from a diverse group such as curriculum specialists. Individual agreements need to be reached by central administration representatives in each discipline as far as the needs of the school in the renovation project. The educational planner needs to permit curriculum specialists to review what has been written and then revise for another review by the same people.

The feedback and review sessions for the community may take a different track. The educational planner should view these meetings as an opportunity to educate the community on the progress of the project and to review what needs were expressed at the previous meetings. The final feedback and review session should present to the community the needs that can be met in the renovation project as expressed previously. This should be a succinct statement that enables the community to understand the scope of the renovation and the extent of their input into the actual project.

The educational specifications for a renovation project should eventually be approved by the school board. If the project is for a complete renovation or renewal of the only high school in the school system, the school board should approve, by formal resolution, the document prepared. In these cases the project will usually entail significant educational program change to warrant school board review. In smaller renovation projects, the school board should simply be informed of the process used to develop the educational specifications and what information is contained in the document.

Renovation Project Content

In a set of educational specifications for a new building many items are discussed relevant to its construction. This document covers everything from playing fields to the amount of storage space inside the building. In a renovation project, much of the same items are covered, but there are some additional items that may be classified as standard. In other words, when a renovation occurs in an existing building new electrical wiring is installed automatically, so is new plumbing. These items are included regardless of what is done to the building as far as the educational program is concerned. Appendix B contains a sample listing of the general scope of a renovation for an elementary school building. These items are included in the set of educational specifications under the heading of ''Special Considerations''. In addition, changes and improvements to the building as a result of the educational program will be stated. These changes can be, for example, the removal of walls to create different spaces, changes in location of disciplines, additions to the building to accommodate new programs, or improvements in equipment. Any change or improvement to the structure of the building should be included in the document.

REFERENCES

Castaldi, B. 1994. *Educational Facilities: Planning, Modernization, and Management.* Boston: Allyn and Bacon, Inc., p. 438.

Earthman, G. I. 1992. Planning Educational Facilities for the Next Century. Reston, VA: Association of School Business Officials, p. 238.

Graves, B. E. 1993. *School Ways: The Planning and Design of America's Schools.* NY: McGraw-Hill, Inc., p. 237.

CHAPTER 7

Complying with Federal Regulations

INTRODUCTION

THE Federal Government through the Congress initiates legislation every year that affects the public schools in some manner. Even though the Federal Government has no direct constitutional responsibility for the education of children throughout the country, there are considerable legislative initiatives that do address the needs of education and, in fact, mandate local school systems to provide certain educational programs. There has been a tremendous increase in the amount of legislation enacted in the past three decades that influences, either directly or indirectly, the public schools of this country. The manner in which schools are organized and administered, plus the educational programs themselves, have changed considerably over this period of time as a result of enacted legislation.

Other segments of the total legal framework in the United States impact the local school system just as finitely as the legislative branch. The legal framework of this country consists of the following parts:

- constitutional provisions
- federal laws
- federal rules and regulations covering legislation
- state laws
- state rules and regulations
- local school board policies
- court decisions, orders, and legal opinions
- decisions of due process hearings of panels established by federal or state legislation

All of these sources of legal compliance and guidance serve to mold the work of the school board and employees to insure equal educational opportunity to everyone regardless of condition or attributes and, at the same time, to provide programs deemed necessary to meet the educational goals of the nation, states, and local school systems.

There are two main areas of legislation that directly impact the local educational program setting. The first concerns the establishment of educational programs that the local school system can and should offer because a federal need is perceived and appropriate funding is offered. These programs are actual instructional programs in which students participate and are usually offered under the umbrella of the General Welfare Clause of the United States Constitution. Under this provision, the government can provide any type of educational program that is perceived as being for the benefit and welfare of the population. A classic example is the 1958 National Defense Education Act in which public schools were offered funds to conduct improved programs in mathematics and science because the country needed more and better prepared scientists to compete successfully with other countries in exploring space.

The Elementary and Secondary Education Act of 1965 and the successive legislation extending that act into the 1990s is another example of legislation establishing educational programs in the public schools under the General Welfare Clause. Under this legislation, Chapter 1 funds are provided to permit instruction in reading and arithmetic to students with limited opportunities because it is in the best interest of the country to help all students be equally prepared. All of the legislation providing funds for vocational education programs and services, beginning with the Smith-Hughes Act of 1917, are other examples of direct funding for instructional programs in the local school system to support a national need (Kimbrough and Nunnery, 1988). During the last two or three decades, federal legislation has been such that the local school system has no alternative than to offer these programs because the wording of the legislation mandates the school system to provide certain kinds of educational opportunities.

Another area of legislation that heavily impacts the activities of the local school system are those laws guaranteed under the United States Constitution and its amendments that deal with the personal liberties of individuals. Legislation on this subject defines certain individual or class liberties. A classic example of this type of legislation is the Civil Rights Act of 1964, in which the rights of individuals are spelled out quite explicitly. Legislation of this order deals with the rights of individuals and classes of individuals as perceived by the Congress under various constitutional provisions and is thought of as an extension of or interpretation of those constitutional provisions. All of the legislation dealing with individual rights impact heavily upon the manner in which the schools are organized and operated. The rules and regulations developed by the various departments of the government to make the legislation operational determine how the school system must treat students. These interpretations guide the school administrator in determining which students will be able to attend school, how and when a student locker can be searched, and what classroom a student will be assigned to for instruction. These regulations also guide the school board and administrators in developing the policies, rules, and regulations they can use to administer the schools. Even the place where students can and cannot attend school is influenced by the interpretation of this type of legislation.

The state and federal court systems, as part of the national legal system, also have an impact upon how, when, and why the school system and its employees act in regards to students and those working for the system. Court decisions about the interpretation of legislation serve to govern local school systems as effectively and permanently as direct legislation. Recent court decisions regarding prayer in the public schools, for example, have caused educators to abandon the use of established prayers at various public gatherings such as graduation exercises in order to comply with the provisions of the United States Constitution.

All of the above types of legislation, and court decisions regarding interpretation of legislation and constitutional provisions, serve to mold the manner in which the public schools operate and treat employees and students. The United States Constitution does make provision for the equal treatment of all individuals who live in this country. In trying to comply with these constitutional provisions and subsequent legislation, the public schools react in certain ways, such as developing their own indigenous policies, rules, and regulations, establishing an educational program, or modifying the physical environment for the individual. In regard to the latter activity, the school system in the past has placed considerable emphasis on providing school facilities that allow all students to participate freely in the programs and activities of the school system no matter where they are offered, and must continue to do so in the future.

SPECIAL LEGISLATION

The intent, implication, and application of all legislation, both on the state and federal levels, the departmental rules and regulations promulgated to enforce that legislation, the court and legal decisions regarding legislation and constitutional interpretation, and local school board policy apply to all students and employees in the school system regardless of condition or other attributes. There is, however, a body of legislation especially designed for persons with disabilities that has a profound influence upon the physical environment that the school system must establish and provide in order to guarantee educational opportunities for everyone. These legislative acts were passed by the Congress of the United States to insure that persons with disabilities would not be discriminated against because of their disabilities and also that they have access to all educational programs and services offered to persons without disabilities. Because these legislative acts have such an impact upon school building design, it is important to review these separately to provide guidance concerning what an administrator needs to know about the requirements the school system must meet in providing an adequate physical environment.

Since the Civil Rights Act of 1964, it has been illegal to discriminate because of the race, religious beliefs, color, or national origins of an individual. This act did not, however, specifically prevent discrimination against an individual with physical, mental, or emotional disabilities. It was not until the Americans with Disabilities Act of 1990 (ADA) that discrimination against a person with disabilities became illegal. Specifically, the ADA prevents discrimination because of disabilities. Because physical disabilities are covered by this act, it becomes important for educators to realize how its provisions impinge upon the school buildings used to educate children.

There are other legislative enactments that specifically state the rights of individuals with disabilities in regards to accessibility to programs, activities, and services. Most of these acts carry some sort of provision for access to the physical environment and these provisions have serious implications for school facilities. Two examples are the Rehabilitation Act of 1973 (P.L. 93-112) and the Education for All Handicapped Children Act of 1975 (P.L. 94-142), and its amendments in the Individuals with Disabilities Education Act (101-476). These two pieces of legislation, joined by the Americans with Disabilities Act, constitute a triad of landmark legislation that has had significant and progressive impact upon school buildings. Each piece of legislation advances the cause of anti-discrimination against individuals with disabilities and adds to a comprehensive pattern of activities initiated to enable these individuals to fully participate in an appropriate educational program, in buildings that do not discourage their participation. For instance, the Rehabilitation Act establishes the concept of removing architectural barriers to and providing accessibility of programs for individuals with disabilities.

THE REHABILITATION ACT

One of the most forward-reaching pieces of federal legislation to impact the public schools is the Rehabilitation Act of 1973 (P.L. 93-112), especially Section 502 which deals with the elimination of architectural barriers in public facilities and Section 504 which mandates accessibility to educational programs. The accessibility concept is enunciated in Section 504:

> No otherwise qualified handicapped individual—shall, solely by reason of his/her handicap, be excluded from the participation in, be denied the benefits of, or be subject to discrimination under any program or activity receiving federal financial assistance.

Almost every school system in the country receives some sort of financial assistance from the Federal Government and as a result, are covered by this section of the act. This provision guarantees students with disabilities access to all programs, services, and activities of the school regardless of the disability. Accessibility, under this act, does not mean that all parts of the existing building must necessarily be accessible, as is the case in new construction, but that the education program must be accessible to the student with disabilities at all times. In the instance where a student cannot physically go to a certain location in the building, the program must then be brought to the student, if the building cannot be made physically accessible. This can mean the possible change of location for any and all programs, including those programs that need special equipment or utilities. For example, if the chemistry laboratory is located on the second floor of a school building and an elevator either is not available or cannot be put into the building and a student with physical disabilities wishes to enroll in a chemistry class, the chemistry program would have to be brought to the student, but the program must be equal to that provided all other students. This could well mean re-location of the chemistry laboratory to part of the building accessible to the student. This type of accommodation is considered "making the program accessible." Of course there are many conditions to be met in the above example, but it gives an idea of how accessibility can mean change of location to allow accessibility to the program.

Section 502 of the Rehabilitation Act mandated the elimination of physical and communication barriers in all public buildings, including schools, where federal funds were used. As a result, the American National Standards Institute (ANSI) incorporated specifications governing the design of facilities to be used by individuals with disabilities. The first ANSI specifications were formulated in 1961 and have since been periodically revised to accommodate newer legislation. These specifications have served as a basis for the design of many school buildings.

In 1984, four agencies of the Federal Government – the Departments of Defense, HUD, the GSA, and the Postal Service – formulated Uniform Federal Accessibility Standards (UFAS) to be used by these departments in designing buildings under their jurisdiction. These rules and regulations were later adopted by the Department of Education. The UFAS is considered more stringent than ANSI standards. In December, 1990, other governmental agencies rewrote their regulations by citing the UFAS rather than ANSI (Tucker and Goldstein, 1993). State and local governmental agencies, as well as private organizations that receive funding from these federal agencies, can apply UFAS and thereby comply with the provisions of Section 504 the Rehabilitation Act.

EDUCATION FOR ALL HANDICAPPED CHILDREN ACT

This act, now known as IDEA, the Individuals with Disabilities Education Act (P.L. 101-476), was passed and signed into law in 1975, and accompanying regulations were promulgated in the Federal Register in 1977. IDEA is considered the most important piece of legislation affecting the education of students with disabilities in the history of the country as far as promoting the educational rights of students with disabilities. Provisions in IDEA do not directly impact physical facilities as much as other legislation, but there are many major provisions in the law which prescribe the way students with disabilities should be treated in the public schools, and by inference have an indirect effect upon school facilities. The most important provisions of the law deal with the development of an Individualized Education Program (IEP), student assessment and evaluation, enactment of procedural safeguards for students and parents, and provision for an education in the least restrictive environment. The latter provision paved the way for more inclusive programs for students with disabilities. Although least restrictive environment and mainstreaming are not the same concept, the idea of a least restrictive environment promotes inclusion of students with disabilities into regular classrooms much more readily and effectively. Least restrictive environment can mean any physical location for a student where that individual can learn effectively with the least restraint. Usually this concept means active association with other students who do not have disabilities and receiving the same quality of instruction as other students. In most cases this means the regular classroom. To extrapolate this idea, the student with a disability would be in the regular classroom as much time as is beneficially possible. In some cases this may be the entire school day. In all cases, the scope of the least restrictive environment is determined individually during the meeting where the Individual Education Program is developed. Least restrictive environment could mean being placed in the regular classroom for one period per day or for the entire day.

Mainstreaming is defined as placing all students with disabilities in regular classrooms with students without disabilities for the entire day. Whatever special instruction or tutoring the student with disabilities might need would be given in the regular classroom. The special education teacher would work with that student in the regular classroom. The only situations where students would be located in special classrooms would be for students with severe or profound disabilities.

The immediate or long-range impact of including students with disabilities in the regular education classrooms, regardless of the length of time, is very minimal, except in particular instances where a temporary overcrowding situation may occur or where special equipment must be moved into the classroom. This slight inconvenience can easily be corrected. The least restrictive environment for students with disabilities and the eventual mainstreaming of almost all students with disabilities does not cause much impact upon the physical facilities of a school system because the total number of students added to the general purpose classrooms is small.

AMERICANS WITH DISABILITIES ACT

The legislation designated as the Americans with Disabilities Act (ADA) prohibits discrimination against individuals with various disabilities. This particular piece of legislation extends the anti-discrimination provisions of previous legislation such as the Civil Rights Act of 1964, the Rehabilitation Act of 1973, and the Education for All Handicapped Children Act of 1975. Whereas Section 504 of the Rehabilitation Act covers organizations that use federal funds, Title II of the ADA extends the anti-discrimination provision to all activities of the school system, as well as all other governmental bodies regardless of the use of federal funds. This act is the most pervasive of the series of legislation regarding individuals with disabilities. Through ADA legislation, the provisions for eliminating physical and communication barriers in buildings, as stated in Section 502 of the Rehabilitation Act, are applied to and mandated for all schools.

Specific provisions of the ADA that affect the physical environment include the following:

> School systems
>
> May not refuse to allow a person with a disability to participate in a service, program, or activity simply because the person has a disability.
>
> Must provide programs and services in an integrated setting, unless separate or different measures are necessary to ensure equal opportunities.
>
> May impose safety requirements that are necessary for the safe operation of the program in question, if they are based on actual risk and not on speculation.
>
> Are required to make reasonable modifications in policies, practices, and procedures that deny equal access to individuals with disabilities, unless a fundamental alteration in the program would result.
>
> Must furnish auxiliary aids and services when necessary to ensure effective communication, unless an undue burden or fundamental alteration would result. (USDOJ, 1992)

In addition to the above provisions, Title II of the ADA provides some guarantees to individual program access that address the accessibility of buildings directly. Some of the more salient highlights are provided below:

> School systems
>
> Must ensure that individuals with disabilities are not excluded from services, programs, and activities because buildings are inaccessible.
>
> Need not remove physical barriers, such as stairs, in all existing buildings, as long as they make their programs accessible to individuals who are unable to use an inaccessible existing facility.
>
> Can provide the services, programs, and activities offered in the facility

to individuals with disabilities through alternative methods, if physical barriers are not removed such as

- Relocating a service to an accessible facility.
- Providing an aide or personal assistant to enable an individual with a disability to obtain service.
- Providing benefits or services at an individual's home, or at an alternative accessible site.

May not carry an individual with a disability as a method of providing program access, except in "manifestly exceptional" circumstances.

Are not required to take any action that would result in a fundamental alternation in the nature of the service, program, or activity or in undue financial and administrative burdens. However, public entities must take any other action, if available, that would not result in a fundamental alternation or undue burden but would ensure that individuals with disabilities receive the benefits or services. (USDOJ, 1992)

The requirement for integrated programs might be one provision that will impact school facilities considerably. One of the fundamental tenants of the ADA is the provision that individuals with disabilities must be included in integrated programs. This has been interpreted to mean that students should be included in all programs of the school or mainstreamed into all aspects of society. This means that students with disabilities who attend public schools must be integrated or immersed into the regular education program. This has been termed "mainstreaming" of special education students into all programs, services, and activities of the school. The ADA prohibits schools from providing services and benefits to students with disabilities through programs that are separate or different, unless, of course, the separate programs are necessary to ensure that the services are equally effective.

Another provision of the ADA pertains to students with hearing, vision, or speech impairments. The ADA mandates that schools must ensure effective communication in all aspects of the school life. Where necessary, the schools may be required to provide auxiliary aids which include such services or devices as qualified interpreters, assistive listening headsets, television captioning and decoders, telecommunications devices for deaf persons (TDD), video displays, readers, taped texts, Braille materials, and large print materials. Most of this equipment and material requires no adaptation of the building other than the availability of sufficient electrical service and appropriate space for the equipment or materials.

The provision for communicating with students with visual impairment may require Braille labeling of all areas of the school building; a visual warning system to augment the bell system announcing class changes and emergencies can be used to communicate with students who are aurally disabled. In addition, the internal and external telephone service should be such that students and employees with disabilities can use these devices effectively. This may mean the lowering of a telephone to accommodate a person in a wheelchair or the provision for special communication equipment for the hearing impaired person. Another feature in the public telephone service would be the provision for emergency services, including 911 numbers, for individuals with speech and hearing impairments. These provisions or requirements are common necessities that cost very little and should always be written into the educational specifications for any renovation, renewal, or modernization project as a matter of public accommodation.

There is a provision in the ADA which states that a school system is not required to provide auxiliary aids that would result in a fundamental alteration in the nature of a service, program, or activity or cause undue financial and/or administrative burdens. Schools must still furnish, however, other auxiliary aids, if available, that do not result in a fundamental alteration or undue burden upon the school system. These two provisions – fundamental alteration or undue burden – are important to school personnel and architects because when a building is renovated, certain structural conditions may result that are not accessible by students who are physically disabled. In addition, certain provisions for assisting students with disabilities may cause an undue financial or administrative burden. This provision does not relieve the school system from the responsibility of providing some sort of aid to enable the student to take part in a program, service, or activity. The burden of finding that solution is, however, upon the school system, not the student.

The ADA stipulates the removal of architectural barriers or structural communication barriers in existing buildings. The definition for an architectural barrier is a physical barrier to access of any kind. A structural barrier to communication is a barrier that is an integral part of the physical structure of the facility. In the latter case, absence of Braille markings or audio alarms, signs out of the visual range of certain individuals, or other situations where communication is not possible, constitute a definition of "structural barriers to communication." In situations where there are such barriers, they should be removed. The following list offers a variety of ways in which these barriers are eliminated:

(*1*) Installing ramps
(*2*) Making curb cuts in sidewalks and entrances
(*3*) Repositioning shelves
(*4*) Rearranging tables, chairs, vending machines, display racks, and other furniture
(*5*) Repositioning telephones
(*6*) Adding raised markings to elevator control buttons
(*7*) Installing offset hinges to widen doorways
(*8*) Widening doors
(*9*) Installing flashing alarm lights
(*10*) Eliminating a turnstile or providing an alternative accessible path
(*11*) Installing accessible door hardware
(*12*) Installing grab bars in toilet stalls
(*13*) Rearranging toilet partitions to increase maneuvering space
(*14*) Insulating hot water lavatory pipes under sinks to prevent burns
(*15*) Installing a raised toilet seat
(*16*) Installing a full length bathroom mirror
(*17*) Repositioning a paper towel dispenser in a bathroom
(*18*) Creating designated accessible parking spaces
(*19*) Installing an accessible paper cup dispenser at an existing inaccessible water fountain
(*20*) Removing high pile, low-density carpeting
[42 U.S.C. Sec 12182(2)(A)(iv); @8 C.F.R. Sec 36.304]

This list is not exhaustive and represents only a small sample of corrective items that could and should be done. All of the above items, however, can be implemented in every building in a school system with little total cost, but the implementation would go a long way in making the building more accessible in addition to complying with the law.

The law also states that the removal of barriers should be readily achievable. "Readily achievable" means that removal can be easily accomplished and carried out without difficulty or great expense. The criteria to be used in making this decision is the nature and cost of the particular action to remove a barrier plus the overall financial resources of the organization. The decision whether or not to remove a barrier is a judgment call on how readily any or all barriers can be removed. In regard to school systems the idea and intent is to accomplish the removal of the barrier, not necessarily to claim exemption because of the difficulty or cost of the removal. When it is impossible to remove a barrier for any of the above reasons – financial or administrative burden or removal not easily achievable – the school system must make the programs, services, or activities available through alternative methods. Such methods may be to bring the program, services, or activities to the individual or to a place in the building that is accessible.

The legislation states that all public entities, including school systems, must operate each program, service, or activity so that when viewed in its entirety, it is readily accessible and usable by individuals with disabilities. If this is not possible the school system must do the following:

(*1*) Remove the barriers to access in that facility
(*2*) Shift the location where the program, service, or activity is provided to an accessible site
(*3*) Provide the program, service, or activity via some alternative method like visits to the home
(*4*) Make alternations to existing facilities
(*5*) Construct new accessible facilities

If structural changes are made in existing buildings to comply with the requirements of the act, they must be completed by January 26, 1995 [C.F.R. Sec 35.150(C)]. Although most of the ADA provisions are now in effect, time constraints for other provisions include the following directives:

1. New construction completed after January 26, 1993 must meet ADAAG standards [42 U.S.C. Sec 12183 (a)(1); 28 C.F.R. Sec 36.401], and
2. Alternations to existing structures made after January 26, 1992 must meet ADAAG standards (28 C.F.R. Sec 36.402).

Key Provisions

There are several key terms or concepts contained in the ADA legislation that should be recognized by educators. These terms deal with decisions regarding the degree of accessibility in a building and apply particularly to renovated or altered existing facilities. Some of these terms have already been discussed in the context of deciding the extent of accessibility in an existing building, but are also identified here for emphasis.

- *Readily achievable*—refers to how easily a barrier can be removed in an existing building. In determining how readily achievable the removal can be, one should consider such things as the nature of the barrier, the cost to remove it, the financial resources of the institution, and the type of operation.
- *Alternative method*—refers to the alternative method by which the programs, services, and activities of a school are made available to disabled persons when a barrier removal cannot be readily achieved.
- *Structurally impracticable*—refers to unique characteristics of the site which might prevent accessibility. These are unusual features such as a building constructed on marshlands or over water necessitating stilts (Battaglia, 1992).
- *Reasonable modification*—(similar to Alternative Method) refers to the change in policies, procedures, and practices that permit a disabled person to participate in the programs, services, and activities of the school.

ACCESSIBILITY COSTS

In designing and constructing a new school building, the General Accounting Office of the United States Government estimates the total additional cost to make that structure barrier-free and to incorporate all of the requirements to aid communication and accessibility is approximately one-half of one percent (.005) of the total cost of the building. On a $20 million high school the cost of accessibility should increase the cost of the building by approximately four cents per square foot of constructed space. Considering the total cost of a new school building, this is not a large amount of funds in relationship to the benefits.

The cost of alteration to make an existing building accessible to persons with disabilities, however, can vary considerably from building to building. Even with the prospect of higher square foot costs of renovation over new construction, the GSO estimates that costs will vary between 0.5–3 percent of the total construction costs for the renovation of an existing building. At the most, this may add approximately $1.20 per square foot to the cost of renovating an existing building similar to the one above.

EDUCATOR RESPONSIBILITY

The big question in dealing with federal legislation concerning accessibility or the specifications for physical features of the building is how much technical knowledge should an educational administrator possess in order to function effectively? In planning for both new buildings and the renovation of existing buildings, the educator needs to know certain things about the legislation under consideration, yet does not need to know the technical specifics of how wide a door should be, the height of a sink, or the proper slope of a ramp in order for a building to conform to required standards for barrier-free environments. The architect and engineer need to have the technical knowledge to design the renovation of a school facility in conformance with building codes. When employing an architect for a renovation project, the school board and administrators need to make certain that the architect and staff to be used in the project have the necessary knowledge of this field as it applies to school buildings. This can be determined at the interview by asking questions about the previous buildings designed and about where the architect gained personal knowledge of the provisions in the law that must be observed in the project. These questions must be raised and answered to the satisfaction of the school board and administrator before a decision to employ is made.

The responsibility of the school board and administrator also extends to a review of the architectural plans to make certain that the resultant renovated building is as barrier-free as possible, or that there is absolute program accessibility if complete physical accessibility is impossible to achieve. Further, the educator needs to know that if there are areas of the renovated building where accessibility cannot be achieved because it is structurally impossible or impracticable, and if accessibility has to be attained through other methods. These methods or options have to be identified and approved by the school board before the renovation project goes to bid. The educator must review the architectural plans with a view to accessibility. This can best be done by studying and reviewing the circulation pathways that a student would normally take to participate in all of the programs, activities, and services of the school. These architectural reviews by educators are crucial in determining the extent of accessibility in a renovated structure.

The responsibilities of the educator in achieving a barrier-free environment in a renovated structure revolve around certain managerial acts. As stated above, the educator does not need to know all of the technical specifications needed to make a building barrier-free, but the educator does need to know how to monitor the processes used in designing the structure. The educator must also know how to supervise the individuals involved, both inside and outside the school system, to make certain they apply their knowledge of the technical specifications called for under the regulations of the law. Specifically, the educator should do the following to properly discharge the responsibility of the school system:

(*1*) Know and understand the general provisions of the law as stated in this chapter

(*2*) Know the timetable and schedule for when accessibility is required under provisions of the law

(*3*) Be able to identify and recommend to the school board competent architects and engineers knowledgeable about the provisions of the ADA and other codes

(*4*) Understand what a barrier is and how to recognize one when reviewing an architectural drawing and evaluating an existing building

(*5*) Be able to intelligently read architectural drawings and plans to determine possible barriers and situations where persons with disabilities would have difficulty

(*6*) Be prepared to raise the appropriate questions to the architect to help ascertain accessibility

By exercising the responsibility of the owner, that is the school board, educators can contribute to the planning, designing, and construction phase of a renovation project and at the same time ensure the final product will conform to the provisions of the law and subsequent building codes.

ARCHITECT RESPONSIBILITY

The architect has the responsibility of designing spaces in an existing structure that will fit the needed educational program. The educator has the responsibility to provide sufficient data describing the type and kind of program that will be carried on in the renovated spaces for the architect to adequately draw a design that will allow for that program to be implemented. In completing the architectural drawings, the architect will draw upon all of his/her body of expertise to create a desirable environment. Part of this expertise is knowledge of building codes and other regulations to which the building must conform. There are several building codes, regulations, and specifications to which a public school structure is susceptible. Some of these codes are federal, some state, and others are local. As a general rule, architects are compelled to adhere to the most stringent set of building codes regardless of the level of government. This means that if the local government's building, fire, and safety codes are more stringent than those of the state and federal governments, or national associations, then the local codes would prevail and be used in designing the building. Approval of the building by fire marshals is usually done on the local level, although there may be a state fire marshal to whom school plans must be submitted for approval. The building permit necessary to begin construction of the facility is issued by the local governmental unit following approval of the plans meeting local building codes. Generally speaking, the local building code is normally seen as the most stringent code. In some of the less populated areas in the country, there are few if any local building codes and in these areas the state uniform building code applies.

Architects are expected to know to which codes and regulations a public school building must conform in order to secure appropriate approvals on both local and state levels. Various standards have been developed in response to federal legislation. Some of the most important standards are the ANSI, ADAAG, UFAS, and ATBCB:

- ANSI – American National Standards Institute – guidelines promulgated by a private organization covering general building standards including disabled access. Used in many schools, but is considered by some as not as stringent as other standards.
- ADAAG – Americans with Disabilities Act Architectural Guidelines – standards developed by the Department of Justice consistent with minimum guidelines developed by the Architectural and Transportation Barriers Compliance Board. To be used by architects in designing schools.
- UFAS – Uniform Federal Accessibility Standards – standards developed by four standard-setting federal departments and agencies for use in enforcing existing rules requiring nondiscrimination on the basis of disability. A very detailed set of standards that clarifies what standards apply in what situations (West,1991).
- ATBCB – Architectural and Transportation Barriers Compliance

Board – Developed a set of recommendations for supplements to the existing UFAS that would apply to environments used by children. Contained in *Recommendations for Accessibility Standards for Children's Environments* (U.S. ATBCB, 1992).

All of the above guidelines or standards can be used in the design of a renovation project for an existing school building; however, public institutions, including public schools, may choose between either the UFAS or the ADAAG. This is because of the application of the ADA upon the schools. Educators should be knowledgeable about the existence of these sets of standards and make inquiry as to which set of standards the architect will be using in the particular project. It is the responsibility of the architect to know and understand the standards and know which set to apply to the project under design.

SOURCES OF ASSISTANCE

There are many offices that can assist the local school system in finding out more about architectural standards and how they affect the local school system. The sources that are most relevant to renovation projects include:

- U.S. Department of Justice
  Americans with Disabilities Act Information Line – (202) 514-0301 – Answers general questions about the ADA law.
- Architectural and Transportation Barriers Compliance Board – (202) 653-7848 – Information about accessibility guidelines for ADA.
- Department of Education
  Clearinghouse on Disability Information – (202) 205-8241 – Provides general information about disability programs.

REFERENCES

Americans with Disabilities Act (ADA). 1990. Public Law No. 101-336, codified at 42 U.S.C. Sec. 12101.

Battaglia, D. H. 1992. *The Impact of The Americans with Disabilities Act on Historic Buildings and Facilities.* Washington, D.C.: Hunton & Williams. Presentation to the Preservation Alliance of Virginia, November 14, 1992, p. 20.

Kimbrough, R. B. and M. Y. Nunnery. 1988. *Educational Administration: An Introduction.* New York: Macmillan Publishing Company, p. 546.

Mayer, C. L. 1982. *Educational Administration and Special Education: A Handbook for School Administrators*. Boston: Allyn and Bacon, Inc., p. 382.

Tucker, B. P. and B. A. Goldstein. 1993. *Legal Rights of Persons with Disabilities: An Analysis of Federal Law.* Horsham, PA: LRP Publications.

U.S. Architectural and Transportation Barriers Compliance Board. 1992. *Recommendations for Accessibility Standards for Children's Environment.* Technical Report. Washington, D.C.: USATBCB, five chapters and appendices.

U.S. Department of Justice. 1992. *Title II Highlights.* Washington, D.C.: Civil Rights Division, USDOJ.

West, J., ed. 1991. *The Americans with Disabilities Act: From Policy to Practice.* New York: Milbank Memorial Fund, p. 360.

CHAPTER 8

Selection of and Working with the Architect

INTRODUCTION

ONE of the most influential persons in determining the success of a planning effort for any capital improvement project is the architect. Regardless of what the project happens to be, the architect is the person who will translate the desired specifications into actual teaching/learning spaces. As such, the time and resources expended by the school system to select a well-qualified architect are worth it. The success of the project can rest with the architect because, unless the desires and needs of the users of the facility are incorporated successfully into the structure in such a way that the building actually works, the users will have to live with the mistakes in the building for the life of the structure.

In selecting an architect for a new building, school systems quite often want the architectural firm to have experience in designing such a project. Further, the school system may wish the firm to have experience in designing a certain grade level building before they are awarded a commission. Likewise, school systems need to find architects with experience in renovation work before a contract is negotiated. The problems in renovation work are so unique and different from new construction that this requirement or criteria should be the first one to which architectural firms must comply before being considered further.

METHODS OF SELECTION

There are several methods by which a school system can select an architect. The most commonly used methods are direct selection, comparative selection, and design competition. There are, of course, some variations in these methods, but basically these are the methods school systems can use.

Direct selection of an architect is a method whereby a pre-determined architectural firm is contacted by the school system and requested to provide some services. Under this method, perhaps only one firm is considered, usually because the architectural firm has done previous work for the schools. This selection method supposes a previous review of the credentials of the firm for initial selection. On subsequent projects, informal evaluations of previous work are made by the staff to decide if the school system should employ the same firm again. In small communities where architectural services are limited, this method of selecting an architect is probably the one most often utilized.

There are some benefits to this method of selection, centering around the supposition that the architect is knowledgeable about the design and construction of the buildings in the school system and is readily available for work. There are, however, some distinct disadvantages to this method of selection. Direct selection of the same architect can cause some inbreeding in which the same solutions to a building project are used time and time again. This approach is not as bad on renovation projects as it is on new construction and additions to existing buildings. As stated above, experience in renovation projects is quite important in selecting an architect. Further, a school system must guard against the possibility that friendship rather than architectural competence is the basis of selection of the architect. The only way to eliminate this possibility is to open the selection procedure to all available architectural firms.

The design competition method is almost never used to select an architect for a renovation project, unless the building has significant historical value or importance. This is a costly method of selecting an architect because the firm must invest money in the project before selection, with a limited chance of being selected. Most architects do not wish to participate in design competitions for just that reason.

The comparative method of selecting an architect is simply the process of reviewing the qualifications of several firms and eventually selecting the one considered the best for the project. This is exactly what the school system does in hiring any employee, whether classified or professional. This method is a very straightforward approach, but is much more laborious and lengthy than the direct method. The comparative method, however, usually results in the selection of the most qualified architect, and is worth the effort. There are specified procedures that must be observed in using this method of selection.

The school system must first develop a pool of receptive architects to invite to participate in the selection process. This is done by contacting the local or state chapter of the American Institute of Architects for lists of member architects. The list will be a very general compilation of names of members of the organization. This list, however, is the basis of the initial selection. Letters of invitation are sent to every name on the list asking for their interest in designing a renovation project for the school system. In the letter, the school system must state what the project will be, the school building under consideration, time line for the project, special considerations, and a brief description of how the architect will be selected. Sometimes a standardized form requesting specific information will be sent to the architectural firm to complete. This is used to gather selected data of a uniform nature. This then becomes the basis of an evaluation of the firm.

Architectural firms will respond to that invitation by supplying the school system with information about previous experience, successful past projects that relate to the proposed project, capability of the staff, and names of previous clients. In addition, the school system may request selected data on the most recent school project completed such as costs, schedule completion, and quality of material. School system personnel will have to peruse these materials to evaluate the firms for the first round of eliminations. Careful evaluation of this material is not an easy task, but it is not impossible. This evaluation may, at first glance, seem incongruous in that this is a case of one professional evaluating the work of a professional from a different discipline, but this is the accepted method of evaluation. Nevertheless, the evaluation must take place based upon the material submitted. The main thrust of the evaluation would be to determine how successful the architect was in previous renovation projects. This can be determined by questioning the users of the building. In addition, the cost of the project and the timing are both essential elements in making an evaluation.

One school system established the following criteria for the initial review and screening of architectural firms.

(*1*) Prior experience with renovations
(*2*) An understanding of Department of Education procedures
(*3*) Quality of prior work
(*4*) Project team experience
(*5*) Ability to perform on time
(*6*) Ability to be on-site daily
(*7*) Past commitment to E.E.O. and MBP (minority business partnership)

Each reviewer is to rate the firm based upon these criteria using the weighted maximum scores for a total of 100 points. A copy of the evaluation form is included in Appendix C. All of these data go into the final results of developing a short list of architects the school system is interested in interviewing.

A short list of three to five preferred architects is developed as a result of the initial evaluation. Once the short list is developed, the school system personnel should gather further data, which can be done by visiting some of the projects the architect has submitted as examples of work completed to determine success of the design. The schools should be visited for a first-hand view of the work of the architect; users can be questioned to obtain their impressions.

The visitations are followed by interviews with members of the firms on the short list. Selection is usually made shortly thereafter. In some cases the school board may wish to interview the best two or three firms and make a final decision based upon that experience. This is well within their purview of authority; however, a few minutes or even an hour interview with an architect in a school board meeting does not gain as much information as site visits and user interviews. When such data has been collected by the staff, the school board should undoubtedly rely upon the recommendation of the school staff.

SELECTION CRITERIA

Developing the criteria for selection of an architect is no different than developing criteria for other types of employment. The work required to be done by the architect is the basis for the selection criteria. There are, however, some criteria the architectural profession itself requires of registered architects that should be used by the school system (California SDE, 1984). Among the more basic criteria are the following:

(*1*) Registration and professional reputation
(*2*) Experience
(*3*) Methods of cooperation
(*4*) Qualifications of the staff and location of offices
(*5*) Interest in the project
(*6*) Quality of previous work
(*7*) References

Other criteria may be added to this list. One criterion pertains to the availability of the architect. Some school systems want the architect to have a local office if they are headquartered in places distant from the school system. An outside architectural firm, in this case, would affiliate with a local architectural firm. Most of the time, renovation projects are not large enough to attract out-of-state architects, but occasionally, in highly populated areas, there are projects sufficiently large to attract such firms.

Registration and Reputation

An architect must be registered by the state in which the firm wishes to operate. Registration is easily checked. Most architects who have a good deal of experience and are recognized by their colleagues belong to the American Institute of Architecture. There are reputable architects who are not members of the AIA, however. This should not be a barrier to employment; however, membership does carry a certain amount of recognition. These criteria are both valuable and easily evaluated.

Experience

For renovation projects, the school system should insist upon an architect with experience in designing a renovation project. The completion of such a project indicates that the architect has some experience with the potential problems that can occur in renovation. This does not necessarily guarantee a successful project, but will give assurances to the school personnel that this will not be a first-time experience. It is very costly for the school system to have to pay for the learning experiences of an architect, especially with the unknown factors in a renovation project. Ideally, the school system wants a firm that has done enough renovation and addition work to have already made all of the learning process mistakes and knows what to look for to avoid them. Of equal importance is the fact that the school system should want experienced members of the firm to work on the project. Not all members of the firm may have had such experience; these are the people the school system does not want completing the project. Guarantees of such experience can be worked into the evaluation of all architects.

Methods of Cooperation

The judgment of this criteria is a subjective evaluation on the part of the school system personnel. Cooperation may be seen differently by two people. What is cooperative to one person may not be cooperative to another person. The school system must question previous clients of the architect. This is probably the best method for developing impressions of the firms level of cooperation.

Staff and Offices

The concern here is whether or not the firm will provide sufficient staff to adequately carry this project through to completion on schedule. The architectural firm must indicate to the school system that it has the staff and capability to complete the proposed project. Here the school staff should be concerned with the size of the architectural staff and the expertise in the field of engineering. A listing of the qualifications of design team members and supporting staff will be helpful in evaluating this dimension. The basic judgment is whether or not, in the view of the school staff, the firm has the staff capacity to complete the job, and if the staff is housed in facilities and offices that will enable them to work efficiently. Sometimes a visit to the offices of the architectural firm will enable the school staff to talk with key members of the staff, to observe the size of the staff, and to make an estimate of how the firm operates.

Interest in the Project

This criterion is also difficult to measure objectively, but personal impressions gained through the interview and informal talks with the architect should produce sufficient data to make a judgment. The principals of the firm must show a high degree of interest, otherwise there may be reason to think a high priority will not be given to this project. All architects are interested in obtaining a commission from a school system because of the stability of the job and the opportunity to work for a public agency.

Quality of Previous Work

This criterion refers to the quality of work done on completed renovation projects, additions to existing buildings, or new construction. The school system must be concerned not only with the total cost of a project, but with what was purchased with the funds given to the architect. In addition, school personnel should be concerned with the question of longevity of the project. If a school system is more concerned with the initial cost of the project than its long-term benefits, the result could very well be a renovation project or new building that will not adequately withstand every day use by students and staff over the long term. This, of course, is not the fault of the architect, but does indicate the ability of the architect to work within given resource limitations. If there is any question as to the quality of work on the part of an architect in a renovation project, the school staff should most certainly visit and observe the finished building.

References

Data gathered through interviews with previous clients of the architect will weigh heavily in the final analysis of developing the short list of firms. These data will help the school staff, and eventually the school board, form impressions of how the architect responded to the needs of the school system, how cooperative members of the firm were, whether or not they stayed within the budget, if the architect maintained the established calendar and schedule, and how serviceable the final facility was for the program. Interviews with previous clients are an excellent source of reliable information with which to make an evaluation of the architect.

All of these criteria should be used in evaluating the architectural firms applying for a contract for a renovation project. The systematic gathering of data will assist the school staff in forming a total picture of each firm and thereby enable them to prioritize the list of applicants. Although this process may take quite some time, the effort is well worth it.

When the school staff has made their evaluations and formulated the final candidate or candidates, the school board may want to interview them. The school staff may assist the school board by developing a set of questions to which each candidate should respond. The questions may help highlight some of the expertise of the architectural firm. In addition, the pre-determined set of questions to which every candidate must address will insure uniformity of response and equality in final selection.

THE ARCHITECTURAL CONTRACT

After the school board decides upon the successful architectural candidate, a formal resolution is passed to employ the firm. This resolution must be included in the minutes of the school board in order for that body to legally sign a contract with the architect. Following this action, the legal counsel of the school system draws up a contract for the school board and architect to sign.

The form of the contract for architectural services may take any shape so long as it meets the legal requirements of the state. Large school systems that employ many architects during the course of a year have their own contract form. Such contracts encompass all of the special situations that are in evidence in the school system. This is the best method of contracting for architectural services and local legal counsel can effect such a contract. The American Institute of Architects has developed a generic contract form that members are able to use. If this contract form is used by the local school system, the legal counsel of the school system should modify the contract to fit the immediate situation. According to some sources, in recent years the AIA contract documents have progressively moved the architect further away from the responsibility for project administration. The AIA contract today does not hold the architect responsible for cost, schedule, or maintaining the necessary control over the process required to minimize or avoid the common problems associated with the construction phase. In such cases, the legal counsel of the school board must modify this document to reflect the needs of the school system. For these reasons, an indigenous contract is probably the best route. For a small school system, copies of architectural contracts developed by a larger school system can be obtained from the superintendent and modified to fit the local situation.

ARCHITECTURAL SERVICES

The architectural services offered through either the school system contract of the AIA contract are basically the same; however, the differences may be in the interpretation of the provisions of the document. The basic services offered by architectural firms through a contract are the following:

- schematic design
- design development
- development of contract documents
- bidding monitoring
- construction monitoring
- orientation and evaluation (AIA, 1982)

The schematic phase covers the design development from the general conceptualization of the project to a set of drawings called schematics. These are drawings which, in essence, define the scope of the work. The architect has covered, at the minimum, the major elements of the project during this phase. In a new building project, the schematic design is a set of drawings of the complete building with each area and space within the building designated and identified. The exterior of the building is determined and usually no further changes to the size of the building are allowed after this phase. In a renovation project, initial design drawings are completed as they would be in a new building project. These drawings would include any changes to the interior structure—changes in size, number, and kinds of spaces. In addition, these drawings would detail the work of improving the various systems of the building. Changes in the plumbing, electrical, and heating/ventilation/air conditioning systems are included by means of drawings. The schematic drawings allow an educator to examine the new utility and mechanical systems that will be put in place. This is especially important, for example, to determine if there is sufficient electrical service to accommodate the expected increase in technology in the classrooms. The schematic drawings should be so well defined that any major changes at this stage will not result in additional design fees to be paid by the school system. The importance of detailed examination and approval of these drawings at this stage cannot be underscored enough. To do otherwise would allow the possibility of a facility that does not exactly meet the demands of the educational program.

After the approval of the schematic drawings, the architect refines these drawings through the design development phase. This phase is just what the name implies, the approved design is refined and developed to the point where the drawings can be used as part of the contract documents. The design development phase is the longest period of design because of the detailed work necessary to develop drawings that can be used by a contractor to prepare a bid for construction.

The next phase of work of the architect is the development of contract documents. The documents themselves include a complete set of drawings and a copy of a book called technical specifications. These two documents form the corpus of the term "contract documents." The architect is responsible for the preparation of these. The technical specifications support the set of drawings by exactly describing the materials that must be used to complete the building project as detailed in the drawings. Although the responsibility for writing the technical specifications rests with the architect, the school system has considerable input into what is contained in that document. Where certain hardware, material, or finishes are required by the school to aid in uniformity of buildings throughout the school system, descriptions of those items will be supplied by the school system. In most school systems there is a desire to have uniform building systems in every structure to facilitate ease of maintenance. This means the school system may require a certain type or kind of door and locking system in every building. The architect incorporates these systems into the drawings and technical specifications. This helps the school system to warehouse similar materials and equipment.

The part the architect plays in the bidding process is usually specified in the contract. Usually the architect assists in preparing the bid announcement, in spite of the fact this is the responsibility of the school system. In some small communities, the architect may seek to encourage contractors to bid on the work. The main responsibility of the architect at this phase is to advise the school board on the bid award. The architect is present at the bid opening and will advise the school board regarding the bids. The architect will usually offer advice on whether or not the bid(s) are within the budget, whether or not there are any areas of particular concern, and where there are points that can be negotiated, should this become necessary. The architect could also make a recommendation to the school staff for acceptance of a bid. This advice is usually considered by the school staff when they prepare a recommendation to the school board, which is their legal responsibility.

The role of the architect for monitoring the construction phase of the project is extremely limited to selected, on-site visits. Such visits are usually done by a member of the staff of the architectural firm and usually do not include the architect who actually designed the project. The contract for the architect stipulates certain site visits to insure conformity of the contractor to the contract documents, but these visits do not necessarily include supervision on behalf of the school system. This area of responsibility is the most difficult to administer. The school system often believes there should be more supervision of the project than the architect does. This can lead to some misunderstandings between the two parties. These circumstances can be avoided by clear provisions in the contract.

The best way to avoid conflict over the supervision of a renovation project or any capital improvement project is for the school system to employ its own supervisor. This person is responsible for monitoring the entire renovation project and provides an interface between the school system personnel and the contractor or architect. The supervisor keeps the renovation project on schedule by holding weekly job meetings where problems and potential problems are discussed with the contractor and architect. The supervisor also maintains a daily journal documenting the development of the project. A school system is well advised to employ such a person regardless of the extent of the renovation. A complete job description of a construction supervisor is contained in Appendix E.

Architects usually like to participate in the orientation of a renovated or remodeled facility to help explain the changes and improvements that were made to the building. In a new facility, the architect plays an important part in explaining how the building works and how the educational specifications are integrated into the building. In a renovation or remodeling project, there is still some explanation needed to inform the school staff of the improvements. This is especially true if a new HVAC system is installed, or improved electrical service to the classrooms is provided.

RENOVATION CONSIDERATIONS

A renovation project is quite different from a new building or an addition to an existing building. Although the same architectural principles are used in a renovation project as in new construction, there are certain pre-design activities that are needed before any design work can begin. The pre-design work usually entails an assessment of the building. In writing the contract, the school system must make certain that such as-needed, pre-design surveys are included in the fee of the architect. These fees might be in addition to the normal fees derived from a percentage of the construction cost.

The architect is paid the agreed upon fee on presentation of a proper invoice stating that certain work has been performed. The invoice is treated like any other and is authorized by the school board and paid by the finance department. After execution of the contract, the school board may pay the architectural firm a retainer fee to certify the contract. Payments usually reflect the following schedule of completed phases:

- schematic design – 15%
- design development – 35%
- contract document completion – 75%

- bidding phase—80%
- construction phase—100%

These are cumulative percentages of payment reflecting the amount of work completed and the total amount of fees paid. For instance, by the end of the schematic design stage, 15 percent of the total fee is paid. By the beginning of the construction phase, 80 percent of the total fee has been paid to the architect, representing the major share of the architect's work.

The contractual relationship between the architect and the school board is no different than any other contract with a firm providing goods or services to the school system. The architectural firm works at the pleasure of the school board and the contract can be terminated at any time for good and just reasons—the main reason being the failure to perform the work required by the contract. The interpretation of this clause can mean the school system is not satisfied with the work of the architect. Although it would be an extreme action, architectural firms can be dismissed for such reasons. If a school system provides the architect with a clear and precise set of educational specifications and constantly monitors the work of the architect to see that the specifications are followed, there is never any reason to exercise this provision in the contract.

ARCHITECTURAL FEES

Architects are paid according to a percentage of the construction costs of the project. This means that the architectural firm calculates the fee according to a certain percent of what it costs the school system to build a facility. On a renovation project, the total cost of the work to restore and renovate the building is the basis for fees. The AIA has a sliding scale of percentage points according to the amount of the construction contract. For the most part, these percentages represent what is considered fair payment for the amount of work entailed in a given project. The exact percentage of the negotiated fee is based upon estimates of what a project will cost. If there is $8 million dollars available in the school budget for a renovation project, then that is the amount used to determine the percentage fee of the architect. Some people believe architects should bid upon a project and the school board award the project to the lowest bidder. This is a gross mistake in the use of the bidding process. Architects provide professional services and are employed based upon professional expertise and judgment. As a result, there are no legitimate bid specifications that would be appropriate for securing such services (Wood, 1985). Procuring such services is much like hiring a teacher, in that professional services are being procured.

REFERENCES

American Institute of Architects. 1982. *Standard Form of Agreement Between Owner and Architect.* Washington, D.C.: The American Institute of Architects, p. 4.

The Board of Regents, The University of Oklahoma. 1989. *Architectural Contract.* Norman: The University of Oklahoma, p. 12.

Wood, C. R. 1985. "Competitive Bidding of Architectural Services," *School Business Affairs,* July.

California State Department of Education. 1974. "Form No. SFP-15," Sacramento: Bureau of School Facilities Planning.

CHAPTER 9

Monitoring the Bidding and Construction Phases

BIDDING THE PROJECT

COMPETITIVE bidding is a very formal and sometimes complicated process that governments and agencies utilize to sort out in an equitable manner who will provide goods and/or services. The process itself is quite simple, but following the legal constraints sometimes requires the consultation of an authority in the field. Competitive bidding seeks to provide all vendors with an equal opportunity to secure a contract with an agency or governmental unit. Bidding encourages competitive prices and provides the bid source with the best possible price for the goods or services desired. This form of securing vendors also eliminates the possibility of favoritism in issuing contracts and insures the receipt of good quality materials.

Every governmental unit uses some form of bidding to secure goods and services. School systems have policies directing when and how bidding should take place. In addition, most states have laws concerning this phase of procurement that the school systems must observe. All of the laws and regulations are designed to provide for uniformity and equity of treatment.

School system employees must be guided by both local school board policies and state regulations concerning bidding procedures when determining whether or not a capital project should be publicly bid. At the school system level, the size of project is often the determinant as to whether it must be publicly bid. Most school systems set a minimum dollar amount above which projects must be bid, regardless of what the project is. These amounts can be as little as $25,000. Some school systems stipulate that any renovation or construction project that cannot be completed by the maintenance staff of the school system must be publicly bid. In smaller school systems, this might mean everything outside of some very minor repair work is publicly bid, because the maintenance staff is so small. Such a regulation causes more work on the part of the administrative staff to put the project out to bid, but the process is much more equitable to the public and undoubtedly safer for the school board.

Bidding Documents

The documents that are used by prospective bidders to determine what their bid will be for the work advertised are called the bidding documents, or sometimes the contract documents. As mentioned in Chapter 8, the contract documents consist of copies of the drawings of the building and technical specifications. The drawings consist of at least four sets of drawings, each covering electrical, plumbing, structural, or mechanical (HVAC) work. The technical specifications consist of descriptions of the material and equipment to be used in construction or renovation. These written materials comprise the necessary documents from which a contractor can formulate a bid.

In compliance with state law, or school board policy, or both, the school system must publicly advertise any capital project to prospective bidders and comply with the provisions of law governing bidding procedures. The type and place of advertisement is also mandated by law. Advertisements must be made in the legal media, which usually is the local newspaper, and stipulated by the school board. In smaller communities, where the legal media has limited circulation, additional bid notices are placed in larger newspapers to provide greater notification around the state or region. On large renovation projects, additional publicity might be given through various trade journals devoted to the construction industry. In certain circumstances, architects may also encourage contracting firms to bid on a project through personal contacts in very small communities. All of this is designed to increase the potential number of bidders and thereby stimulate competition.

Pre-Qualification of Bidders

A school system may require potential bidders to pre-qualify themselves before a bid can be accepted from them. Through pre-qualification, potential bidders can be selected before they submit a bid. It is a method of reducing the pool of bidders to those firms that have the capabilities to complete the project. In a way, the licensure of firms is a pre-qualification because the state will license only those firms which have certain minimum standards of experience, financial stability, and expertise.

School systems can impose other qualifications upon firms before they are allowed to bid. For example, in the case of a renovation project, the firm might have to have prior experience on a similar type and size renovation project. This would be particularly appropriate because of such potential problems as hidden asbestos. Requesting the bidder to demonstrate the capability of handling environmental problems like asbestos abatement would be a justified pre-qualification.

Other pre-qualifications deal with acceptance of and adherence to various parts and provisions of the Civil Rights Act of 1964 and subsequent federal legislation dealing with disabled persons. One interesting pre-qualification enacted by the city of Philadelphia was that potential bidders had to assure the city there was sufficient minority representation on their work force as demonstrated by employment rolls. Sometimes states will give preference to firms located within the state. Such preference provisions are an obtuse way of pre-qualifying a firm because an advantage is given to those firms which happen to be located within the state.

Public Bid Advertisement

The public notification of the project contains a specific date, time, and place where bids will be publicly opened. Members of the purchasing department of the school system conduct a public opening of each bid at the given time, date, and location. Usually representatives of the firms that have submitted bids attend the opening. At the given time all bids received are opened and the amount of each bid is written on a chalkboard or chart for all persons to read. After all bids have been opened and recorded, the school staff and architect confer to determine the lowest responsible and responsive bid.

Responsive and Responsible Bidder

The successful bidder is the company that is considered responsible and has submitted a responsive bid to the school system; the bid chosen must meet these two requirements, but also be lower than all those of the other firms that meet the requirements. Determination of the lowest responsible and responsive bidder is not always an easy task. The lowest bid is easy to determine, but responsibility and responsiveness are not. Sometimes it is necessary to do some searching for data to assess these qualifications.

Responsibility as far as contracting firms is concerned usually refers to the financial strength of the firm. The test of responsibility can be determined by the ability of the firm to obtain bonding. When a contractor submits a bid for a specified project, a bid bond covering 5–10 percent of the total amount of the submitted bid price is required. A bid bond is sometimes referred to as a surety bond because the bond assures the bid to be in earnest. The contractor obtains such a bond from one of the many bonding companies throughout the country by submitting financial information on the firm. The financial data must be healthy or the insurance company either will not insure the firm or will charge a high premium. A high bond premium is likely to be reflected in a high bid.

Another criterion to ascertain responsibility would be the licensure of the firm. The state usually issues a license to builders so the firm can work on many different sized projects. Obtaining such licenses means the firm has supplied the state with certain data relative to its financial stability and the extent of experience the firm has had. In addition, the school system can require each bidder to submit certain data relative to the financial stability of the firm. So long as all of the firms concerned are required to submit these data, the legality is not questioned.

The school system must also assess the history of the firm to determine if it has performed well in the past. Previous work history with the school system should weigh heavily upon the decision to award a contract. A contracting firm may be denied a contract based upon previous work history if its work has been harmful to the school system.

Responsiveness is no easier to determine than responsibility. Obviously, being responsive means the firm has responded to the notification by submitting a bid, but responsiveness also means the bid must be somehow responsive to the resource limitations of the school system and should be competitive with other bidders. A bid that greatly exceeds the resources of the school system is not responsive, unless there are problems in the economy or within the budget figures of the school system.

Rejection of bids is well within the purview of the school board for good and just reasons. Even when the bids are tendered and received, the school board for specified reasons can reject any and all bids. The reason most often cited for rejecting bids is that all of the bids exceed the budgeted amount for the project. There are other acceptable reasons, but usually they center around the availability of resources and/or the needs of the project. In most cases where all bids are above the budgeted amount of funds, the architect and school staff seek ways to reduce the size or scope of the work in order for at least some part of the project to begin. In addition, the cost of the project is negotiated with the most promising bidder to ascertain if the cost of the project can be reduced so that a bid can be accepted and a contract awarded.

Finally, a bid can be rejected by the school board because of previous unsatisfactory work experience with a particular firm. Even if that bid is the lowest on a particular project, a school board may pass over the bid to award a contract to the next highest bidder. The firm can be disqualified because of poor work performance as judged by the school system. This situation rarely happens, yet this is a legal prerogative of the school board.

Contract Award

When the lowest responsible and responsive bid is identified, the school staff makes a recommendation to the school board to accept it. This occurs in the context of a public school board meeting at which time the school board passes a resolution to accept the bid. After that, the legal counsel of the school board draws up a contract to be signed by both the school board and representatives of the firm. When this is completed, the successful bidder deposits with the school board a performance bond equal to 100 percent of the bid. At the same time, the school board returns the surety bond the bidder had given the school board when the bid was first offered. In addition to the performance bond, the successful bidder also gives the school board a payment bond. The payment bond protects the school board from any legal action that might be taken by sub-contractors who the contractor may not have paid by providing funds to pay them directly. This latter bond prevents the imposition of a lien against the building by a sub-contractors who was not fully paid for work done on the project. These two bonds are a legal requirement of the school board to protect itself in case of some financial difficulty on the part of the firm that will be doing the renovation work on the building. Such provision is also considered by the courts to be prudent administration on the part of the school staff.

The contract the successful bidder signs calls for specified work in a building with stipulated materials using good quality workmanship.

Assessing the quality of the work completed and the materials used by the contractor is an easy task that can be done at any time. Simple observation plus certain field tests can determine these, but the latter quality, that of good workmanship, is a judgment that must be made by a qualified person at the time of construction. After the renovation project has been completed is not the time to make an assessment of the quality of work because it is too late for correction. Although the architect has stipulated the work to be completed, the materials to be used, and the quality of work, it is usually up to the owner to determine the actual quality of work as shown in the finished product. Supervision of this part of the project is very important to insure that all work is performed in a manner which guarantees a functional and aesthetically pleasing building upon completion.

CONSTRUCTION SUPERVISION

Initially the responsibility of the school system in providing supervision to a renovation project may seem to be very little. The work and materials are very clearly defined in the contract documents, as is the time line for completion of the work. The school system does, however, have a very compelling interest in and responsibility for the timely completion of the project. As a result, the school system must be aware at all times of the progress of the contractor in completing the project.

The only way the school board can be well appraised of the progress of the renovation project and assured of compliance with the building documents is to have a supervisory employee at the construction site at all times. The person, appropriately titled "construction supervisor," "facility supervisor," or even "construction manager," is to provide close supervision of the work of the contractor to guarantee compliance with and adherence to the contract. This supervisor should have some knowledge of the construction process and materials used in buildings and be able to apply that knowledge to assist the contractor in completing the renovation successfully in a timely fashion.

The supervisor should also conduct a weekly job site meeting between the representative of the architect and the contractor. These meetings provide opportunities to determine the progress of the project, identify any problems or detrimental conditions that may influence the progress of the work, and plan for the future. Potential and actual problems of any nature are discussed at these meetings, and solutions are sought to prevent any disruption of the work. This interface between the school system, architect, and contractor should be the forum for all discussions that will aid in the timely completion of the project.

The importance of the renovation project in improving a school building, plus the large expenditure of public funds, mandate that the project be adequately supervised. Such supervision can be given only if a personal representative of the school board, namely a school system employee, is present every day to make certain the project is completed correctly. The amount of funds expended for proper supervision is indeed small when compared with the total funds expended for the project. By keeping the project on schedule and solving problems as quickly as possible on-site, a good construction supervisor can save the school system more funds than the salary paid for that supervision. For the school system not to provide such supervision is not only poor economy, but also imprudent administration.

CHANGE ORDERS

During the course of a renovation project, it may become necessary to make certain changes in the work to be completed by the contractor. From time to time, school staff may want to include something in the renovation project that was not noted in either the architectural drawings or the technical specifications. Although the school system should always try to be very precise in writing out what changes are needed in the school building, there are times when opportunities to implement new methodology may present themselves after a contract has been signed. To change the building to accommodate such methodology would be in the best interest of the school system. When changes to the contract must be made, the school system must issue this change.

Change orders may also come from certain site conditions. If unanticipated conditions arise when the contractor is working, certain changes have to be made in the contract to enable the contractor to fulfill the contract. For example, a contractor may open a wall section of the building only to find utilities there that had not been noted on the original architectural drawings and had not been anticipated. Removal of such utilities may be an added cost which should not be assessed against the contractor. In such cases, a change order increasing the cost of the contract should be approved and issued by the school board.

Universally, change orders originate either with the school staff or the contractor. The request is reviewed by the architect and if amendments in the form of drawings or technical narrative have to be produced, the architect completes this work. The change order is then approved by the architect and sent to the school staff and school board for its approval. By approving the change order the school board agrees to either increase or decrease the dollar amount of the contract with the contractor accordingly.

The change order involves either the crediting or debiting of funds in favor of the school board, or the contractor as the case may be. Because the work and materials called for in the change order are not publicly bid, costs of a change order are usually high. For this reason, changes in the contract should be minimal. Good architectural drawings, precise technical specifications, and close supervision of the construction process will keep requests for change orders to a minimum.

CONSTRUCTION MANAGER

In recent years there have been a number of firms that have become specialized in managing construction projects; they provide supervisory service for the owner during the construction phase. This service does exactly what the construction supervisor of the school system would do for the school board. In addition, some construction management firms provide additional services such as architectural work and construction services. This could almost be termed a "complete operation" in that all of the architectural, supervision, and construction work is done by one firm. These services relieve the school system of considerable supervisory work associated with the traditional approach to guiding construction or renovation projects.

Although construction management may seem a very comprehensive service to the school systems, there are some distinct disadvantages of this approach. Most of the disadvantages center around the amount of direct control over or input into various processes involved in a capital improvement project. Usually the school system completes the planning and programming for a construction project, regardless of the kind of project. This is followed by selecting the architect, monitoring the design process, publicly bidding the project, selecting the contractor, and then supervising the construction phase. Under a construction management contract, all of those processes are under the control and implementation of a construction management firm. All major construction or renovation projects are publicly bid in accordance with school board policies and state law. In some construction management contracts, the project is not publicly bid. Such arrangements are clearly not in the best interest of the school system and are undoubtedly not legal. School systems must constantly be aware of these situations when contemplating the use of construction management firms to supervise a capital improvement project.

Also, construction management is much more costly than employing a competent person on the school staff to do the same job. Even with fringe benefits and supporting staff for the supervisor, the school system employee is less expensive than a construction management firm for supervising construction. In addition, it is difficult to make an accurate determination of construction management costs. Most school systems do not have the expertise to adequately make such judgments.

Changes in plans are inherent in all construction projects and how these changes are handled is very important. Under construction management methods, design work often proceeds simultaneously with construction activities. As a result, plan review is greatly complicated. Sometimes the design schedule provides little time for adequate review of plans by all concerned school staff members. This is not in the best interest of the school system.

CHAPTER 10

Building Administrator Responsibility during a Renovation

INTRODUCTION

WHEN renovation of a building takes place, the local school staff is heavily involved with the project. In small renovation projects the work can, in most instances, be completed over a summer when students and teachers are absent. This does not cause a dislocation of the student body, nor the imposition of construction activities during the school day. In a major renovation project, however, it may not be possible to relocate the student body to other schools, and the students must occupy the school while repairs and renovations take place. In a renovation project there is considerable internal construction work done. As a result, teachers and students must share with construction workers the immediate area of the building under renovation. In addition, teachers, administrators, and students must also contend with the normal clutter and messiness of construction. These conditions present constant opportunities for problems to arise between the educators, students, and workers. When an addition to a building is constructed, there is usually sufficient separation between the existing building and the new construction to prevent most contact problems. This physical separation prevents the constant interplay between craftsman, educator, and student, which is a nexus of problems.

BUILDING PRINCIPAL RESPONSIBILITY

The principal plays a significant role in preventing, ameliorating, and solving problems between staff, students, and members of the contracting firm during renovation work in a school. The position a principal has in this arrangement is quite unique. The principal is in charge of the building and the people in it. At the same time, the contractor has a contract with the school system to complete certain work under a deadline. But since a school system representative, and not the principal, is the official contact between the school system and the contractor, then the principal must carefully and diplomatically keep peace. When questions, complaints, and suggestions are raised by the contractor, a representative of the firm must work through the official school system contact. The school principal is not the official school system contact for the contractor. In fact, the school principal does not have any control over the contractor. The contractor is an independent agent servicing the school system with certain work. When work is done in a school building, it is necessary for the contractor to work cooperatively with the school staff to insure that the educational program is not interrupted. All of these conditions are stipulated rather clearly in the contract the contractor signs with the school board; the interpretation of the language of the contract on the daily job site, however, is up for discussion and resolution.

The vast majority of the conflicts between staff and workers deals with accessibility to various parts of the building. This can occur when teachers and students cannot use certain spaces during different times of the day or year because of construction activities, or when workers are unable to complete work because of unavailability of work space. The second largest number of problems occur because of program interruption as a result of either noise, workers present, or loss/displacement of material and equipment.

There are occasionally some personnel problems that occur during a renovation project. These problems usually deal with the interface between school employees and construction workers and students and construction workers. As can be expected, the problems arise from some kind of misunderstanding of rights or procedures. Sometimes outside workers may wish to become too friendly with staff and students, and conversely, students may encourage contact with workers. These problems are the most difficult to control and solve, and demand the diligence of the principal in discouraging these situations from the outset. Maintaining a proper and agreed upon work schedule on the part of the contractor helps a great deal in minimizing the contact between the three groups of individuals. Likewise, a well-maintained instructional schedule and strict supervision will go a long way in preventing contact.

Workers are usually made aware by their employers of the need for physical separation between the school staff, students, and themselves, but the application of this is still difficult because of the fact that the school is trying to operate at the same time that reconstruction is taking place. In addition, the construction firm has certain schedules to adhere to, and this puts pressure on the workers to complete their tasks by a certain time or date, regardless of who is occupying the space. Coupled with this is the natural attraction and interest by students towards outsiders. The best mode of operation is, of course, to eliminate such problems before they begin. This can be done by reaching an understanding with the contractor, in the case of the workers, of what will happen to the various parties should a problem arise. In the case of a worker it could well mean loss of job or at least banishment from the work site. The school staff and student body should also be appraised of how they are to act and the consequences should they initiate contact. The possibility of unwanted attention towards a student or students on the part of a worker is something the principal does not want or need because of serious repercussions throughout the community and school system. Such problems can accelerate to official complaints unless they are solved immediately at the school level. Only by constant monitoring of the students and workers can such problems be either minimized or eliminated.

Some school systems schedule the contractor to do the actual renovation work on the building in the evening when there are no students. Work typically begins after the school is empty and ceases late at night. Such an arrangement allows the workers greater freedom in doing their work and at the same time allows the teaching staff to work uninterrupted by workers and machinery. Many space and personnel problems are eliminated by this routine. Although this may result in higher construction costs, the reduction of problems is well worth the effort. School systems stipulate this provision in the bidding document so that prospective bidders are aware of working conditions before being awarded a contract.

When a problem does occur, the principal and staff must act quickly to resolve it by communicating their concerns to the person in charge of the workers. If the problem can be solved by a friendly warning to the worker or student, so much the better. For more serious problems, however, some form of data gathering and possibly a hearing conducted by the principal is required. The main point here is that the principal is officially in charge of the building and everyone who is in the building. This means that the rules and policies set by the principal and administrative staff must guide and govern the conduct of everyone in the building, including the workers. Granted, the workers are not employees of the school system and their allegiance is to the contracting firm either through union contract or through employment agreements, but they must observe the rules of conduct established by the principal in cooperation with the representatives of the firm. Adherence to such rules will ensure the orderly progression of work throughout the project and permit employees of the construction firm to enter into such areas as needed to complete the project.

When a renovation project starts in a school building, the principal must appoint someone to be the main contact person with the school system representative. In a large school, this person is usually appointed from the administrative staff of the building. The appointee should have the authority of the principal to make independent decisions that will not cause problems later. In smaller schools, the principal may well be the main contact person. In these situations, the principal must assume these responsibilities in addition to the regular demands and requirements of administering the educational program. The main responsibility of the principal is to see that the educational program is not interrupted and the students and staff are protected from possible harm.

The local school building representative meets with the school system representative, construction supervisor, architect, and contractor when necessary. In most large renovation projects, there are weekly job site meetings with a representative of the central administration who may be a member of the facilities department, the director of maintenance and operations, a construction supervisor, or someone charged with the responsibility of monitoring the renovation project. In addition, representatives of the architectural firm and the contractor attend the weekly job site meetings. The school system representative calls the meetings, conducts them, and maintains the minutes. These individuals or their representatives meet every week to discuss the progress of the project. During the course of the meetings, the contractor will detail the work that was completed during the previous week and that anticipated during the coming week. The contractor will also stipulate those areas of the building in which work will take place and situations that may cause some disruption to the educational program. Schedules for activities are then developed and agreed upon so that both the school principal and the contractor understand what arrangements need to be made in the school routine and/or changes in the work program of the contractor.

In all of these arrangements, the school staff should not hinder the contractor unnecessarily from working at a pace that will enable the firm to complete the project. Unnecessary delays of the contractor will inconvenience the school staff in the future, and therefore, should be avoided at all costs. At the same time, the work of the contractor must not impede the progress of the educational program, because the main responsibility of the school system is to maintain the educational program at all times. Comfortable compromises between school staff and workers where necessary will enable the school staff to keep the educational program operating at a high level of effectiveness and at the same time allow the contractor to meet contract deadlines. A delicate balance of needs must be maintained so that both the school and contractor can meet goals with a minimum of interruption and inconvenience. Sometimes great skill in diplomacy is needed by the school building principal or representative to effect this balance, but whatever it takes, this balance must be maintained for the benefit of all parties.

SITE-BASED MAINTENANCE PROGRAMS

The public schools throughout the country traditionally have been associated with the concept of central administrative decision making. This application originated for a variety of reasons, but primarily from the need to have control over a large organization and to bring uniformity of application to an organization with many sites. This model has served the public schools well in the past by introducing and internalizing some efficient administrative practices into local organizations. For the past decade, however, some administrators have felt that decision making should be closer to the action. To these administrators it is beneficial to the educational process to have decisions made as close to the student as possible with the anticipation that local resource disbursement will positively affect learning. Further, it is believed that local allocation of funds provides greater efficiency and allows for more flexibility in application of resources.

Site-based management of schools is an alternative organizational arrangement to the hierarchical school system governance arrangement where decision-making power is lodged in the central administration. It is generally defined as a system where the individual school building is the locus of educational decision making. In site-based management, the responsibility for making decisions is the responsibility of either the building principal, faculty, or community members, or any combination of the three. In some cases even students are involved in the decision-making process.

This kind of alternative organizational arrangement has been implemented in many school systems throughout the country. The exact arrangement, however, varies considerably from locality to locality, depending on how the local educators or school boards conceptualize site-based management, or how state or local statute defines this type of organizational pattern. The variety of application extends from one extreme to the other. In some instances, site-based management is in name only, whereas, in a single building organization, such as a private school, site-based management is the only organizational pattern available.

Site-Based Administration

The hallmark of almost every site-based management application is the local authority over three aspects of administration: budget, curriculum, and personnel. These three functions have to be explained and operationalized in some form in any plan for decentralization of decision making or devolution of power. Site-based budgeting assumes that local personnel are better informed about the resource needs of students and can expend funds in a more efficient manner than through a central administrative office. In some of the more distinct applications of site-based budgeting, local school staffs are allowed to determine how a given lump sum of funds is distributed for personnel, equipment, supplies, and even maintenance.

Site-based curriculum development refers to decisions made regarding subject matter offered or methodological application. The belief here is that principals, teachers, and parents working together can produce the necessary results in students and meet their educational needs more accurately than can a director or supervisor from a central office. Personnel decisions in site-based management schemes are based upon the idea that the local school organization should choose what kind of staff to employ if the school staff is to be held accountable for student performance.

Site-based management is considered a significant trend in American education today; every school system in the country will deal with it in some fashion. A school system may choose to ignore the trend and continue in their present operation, whatever that may be. There are those school systems, because of their small size, that have always operationalized a site-based management concept simply because that is the best and probably the only way to operate. The larger school systems, however, are the ones that must confront the issue. These school systems must decide whether or not site-based management, regardless of method, will be put into practice. In some cases, state governments have mandated site-based management schemes. Of course, there has always been a certain degree of site-based management in all school systems, even in the most centralized organizations. Local implementation of site-based management has always been a matter of definition and degree.

Whatever the definition of site-based management in the local school system, the actual areas of responsibility and decision making need to be negotiated. In other words, the central administration and the local school building administration need to come to some agreement as to what decisions are to be made on the local building level and which are reserved for central administration. Of course, the actual locus of decision-making regarding the three areas of concern will vary in each jurisdiction, but this is the first step in implementing site-based management. State mandates will influence how much decision making authority the local school building staff will have in matters involving the curriculum. In addition, union contracts may impact the level of decision making authority the school building staff has. The amount of school building decision making in budgetary matters will rest on the school board and its interpretation of state fiscal regulations. All of this, however, needs to be taken into account in developing a site-based management system. Empowerment of the local school staff has to come about as a result of negotiations of areas of responsibility.

Implementation of site-based budgeting will entail many facets of administration because of the need for resources to maintain certain levels of program offerings, staff availability, and deployment across the school system. Local school building staff may be given very little authority in expending funds on these matters, and yet, some staffs may be given great latitude and be subject to certain resource allocation formulae and accounting procedures of the central administration.

Site-Based Funding

An additional area of great concern in budgetary areas that is usually addressed in site-based schemes is that of funding the school system maintenance program. The maintenance program covers every school building owned and operated by the school board. Preserving the initial investment of the community in every local school building is a very important responsibility of the school board. This body is charged with keeping each building, as much as possible, in as good a state of repair as when it first opened. This is a difficult task to complete, given the limited resources available to the school board. To complete this task, persons with expertise in the area of building maintenance are employed by the school board. These staff members are very expert in keeping the school buildings in good working condition. Maintenance employees are usually deployed and directed by the central administration staff.

The centralization of the maintenance function of the school system has been seen as beneficial for several reasons. First of all, the limited resources available can be applied in a uniform manner to all of the needs of the inventory of buildings of the school system. In other words, each school building is treated equally and fairly in regards to maintenance needs and resource availability. In those school systems that have a centralized maintenance schedule, equal resources will be allocated and maintenance needs addressed for each building on a regularly scheduled basis. Unfortunately, in some school systems a regularly scheduled maintenance plan that addresses these building needs in a systematic fashion is not in place. In these cases, maintenance needs may not be taken care of in an equal and fair manner, but rather as need arises. As a result, not all maintenance needs may be addressed nor preventative maintenance implemented. For the most part, however, a centralized maintenance program can provide for an equalization of resource utilization and a uniformity of practice.

The second benefit of centralized maintenance is that the building administrator is relieved of the responsibility for completing the maintenance work that is always evident. The principal is the expert in administering the school educational program and personnel, and that task takes the full effort of the administrator to accomplish. On the other hand, the process of identifying maintenance needs and then doing those tasks required to get the work done, is beyond the realm of responsibility of the building principal. To identify, schedule, and satisfy maintenance needs, the school board employs experts and selected craftsmen who can handle these projects. This arrangement is a sort of divided administrative responsibility based upon expertise in the position.

LOCAL SCHOOL BUILDING INVOLVEMENT

There are instances where the building principal and staff should have strong input into scheduling the completion of certain maintenance projects. These situations are where the maintenance item has some impact on the curricular program or the health and safety of the students and staff. In these cases, the building principal and staff should have a strong voice concerning the decision of when the project is to be completed. Most school systems regularly, as a matter of policy, involve the principal, staff, and even community representatives in identification and scheduling of maintenance projects in the overall, district-wide, maintenance list. For the most part, such arrangements serve the needs of the school building staff by completing those projects they want to have done, as well as accomplishing the building maintenance needs as seen by the central staff.

Under site-based management schemes, decisions regarding maintenance needs might well become negotiable. This would mean that the extent of decision making of the principal and staff as far as maintenance projects to the building are concerned would be determined cooperatively with the central administration and eventually the school board.

Negotiating Division of Responsibilities

The real question to be posed, however, is how much of the maintenance function should be the responsibility of the local school staff and how much the central administration. The maintenance function is much more than simply deciding which project, out of a list, to fund or not to fund, although that decision is quite important in getting the job done. There are at least six different processes involved in properly maintaining school property: (1) identifying the condition to be repaired, corrected, or maintained; (2) specifying or describing the method of repairing or correcting the condition and assigning a level of funding to complete the task; (3) scheduling the work to be done; (4) publicly bidding the project and awarding a contract to an outside contractor or assigning a school employee or team to complete the work; (5) inspecting and monitoring the work of either the outside contractor or school system employee; and (6) certifying that the work was done satisfactorily and reporting back to the proper authority.

Some of these processes may not be within the desired range of authority of the school building staff in a site-based management scheme, but they must all be done by some office or person in the school system. Responsibility for completing these processes or tasks must be placed upon competent persons and must be aligned in such a manner to assure proper continuity towards completion of each project. Deciding who or what office should assume these responsibilities then becomes the focal point in the division of labor between site-based management and central administration when the negotiations take place. Negotiations need to lead to the determination of responsibility for maintenance processes between either the central administration or the site-based management team. When negotiating these responsibilities, some very difficult questions need to be answered such as the following:

(*1*) How will maintenance funds be equitably allocated to individual school buildings? On what basis—per pupil, square feet, or building need?
(*2*) Will building principals and staff make the final determination of how maintenance funds will be expended?
(*3*) Who or what group will identify maintenance needs of the building?
(*4*) How will the school system achieve economy of scale/volume in bidding projects (i.e., grouping like items for one bid; buying in bulk; obtaining similar services for more than one site. . .)?
(*5*) Who will be allowed to tender bids for maintenance projects?
(*6*) What maintenance projects will be bid by the building staff or by the maintenance department?
(*7*) How can the school board guarantee adherence to proper legal procedures when projects are bid on the building level?
(*8*) Can building principals sign valid contracts for goods and services used in maintenance projects? If so, for what amount?
(*9*) Can principals use funds from sources other than the school system to complete maintenance projects? For example, PTA funds, Band Boosters, Quarterback Club, Pep Club, etc.
(*10*) Who is responsible for inspecting the work of the contractor if the central administration maintenance department does not bid the project?
(*11*) What appeal process is in place to insure that differences between local building and central administration can be resolved in an equitable manner?
(*12*) What kind of staff development will need to be given to the local school building decision makers to help them become knowledgeable about maintenance needs, priorities, and processes?
(*13*) How can the school board guarantee preventative maintenance tasks are completed in a regular and timely fashion if the local

school building is making decisions regarding how funds are expended?

(*14*) What kind of staff will the school building principal need to properly take care of all maintenance projects?

When these questions are answered to the satisfaction of both the building and central administration, the school board can feel reasonably assured that the maintenance program of the school system will function properly and will maintain all buildings in a good state of repair. The school board, of course, is interested in making certain that a quality maintenance program is conducted in a professional manner to insure the safekeeping of all buildings. Through a definition of responsibilities and subsequent allocation of authority and funding, the maintenance program can succeed. This is the only way the school board can be assured that this important administrative responsibility will be fully and appropriately discharged.

REFERENCES

AASA, NASSP, and NAESP. 1988. *School-Based Management: Strategy for Better Learning*. Arlington, VA: AASA; Alexandria, VA: NAESP; Reston, VA: NASSP, p. 22.

Clune, W. H. and P. A. White. 1988. *School-Based Management: Institutional Variation, Implementation, and Issues for Further Research*. New Brunswick, NJ: Center for Policy Research in Education, p. 42.

Davies, B. and L. Ellison. 1990. "Local Management of Schools: The Current Revolution in English Education," *School Business Affairs*, 56(5):16–23.

Honeyman, D. S. and R. Jensen. 1988. "School-Site Budgeting," *School Business Affairs*, 54(2):12–14.

Kubick, K. 1988. "School-Based Management," ERIC digest Series, Number EA 33, ERIC Clearinghouse on Educational Management, 1988, p. 2.

Pierce, L. C. 1977. *School Site Management*. Cambridge, MA: Aspen Institute for Humanities, Program in Education for a Changing Society, pp. 1–23.

CHAPTER 11

Evaluating the Renovation Project

INTRODUCTION

WHEN the renovation project is completed, it is necessary to evaluate the outcome of the work. For the building evaluation, a set of procedures and tools are used to determine the strong and weak points of a newly renovated structure and to inform the school board of how well certain design features work in the building (White, 1992). The renovation of a building is designed to bring that structure up to some pre-determined standards, whatever they may be. In some school systems, the goal of the renovation effort is to equalize the educational opportunity for all students by providing similar physical surroundings in all school buildings. In other words, the older buildings should have comparable physical spaces, equipment, and accoutrements needed for the educational program as are in the new buildings. Equity can be determined even though the spaces may not look exactly the same.

Typically, when a capital improvement project or new building is completed, educators are so pleased to have the facility in operational order, they give little thought to evaluation of the facility. In addition, a new building represents the newest and best of facilities the school system has to offer. For this reason, formal evaluations of capital projects are usually not done; however, it must be remembered that some data are available only at the period of completion of the project and, consequently, must be gathered at that time.

Two things need to be evaluated in a renovation project—the product and the process. The product of the renovation project is the completed building and how it works. The process is the planning—the many activities various individuals and groups of individuals involved did to bring about the completed project. Both the product and the process of planning are legitimate subjects for evaluation (Earthman, 1991).

PRODUCT EVALUATION

The finished product of the renovation project is the renovated or improved building. Although the prime evaluation point is the usefulness of the building, there are some basic parameters or criteria against which the renovated structure should be evaluated. The decision to renovate any building is always predicated upon cost factors, i.e., the cost of renovating an existing building compared to the cost of constructing a new facility. Other factors such as programmatic and time were considered in making the final decision. Therefore, part of the evaluation should address these factors. The following factors that were considered in the initial decision making should be evaluated again using post-construction data:

- cost per square foot
- cost per pupil
- amount of square feet of space allocated per pupil
- numbers and cost of change orders
- construction time
- staff time and effort

These very important considerations will help a school system adequately judge how cost effective the project was and how the latest project compared with previous renovation projects in terms of overall costs and proposed costs of a new facility. Naturally, historical comparisons of the costs of renovation projects will better enable the school staff to predict costs for future projects. In this manner, unit costs more reflective of the market and practice can be used in future capital budgets.

The evaluation of a renovation project should not be limited to cost analyses. What is vitally important is the question of how well the renovated building accommodates the given educational program (Macclay and Earthman, 1992). Evaluation of a renovation project is somewhat different than that of a newly completed building, although both evaluations use the educational specifications as the basis of the judgment. The basis of or reason for a renovation is that the building needs to be brought up to the level of the newest building in the school system. In other words, the old building should reflect all of the new features that are incorporated into the newest building.

In a new building there are little if any physical constraints to implementing the educational specifications, which in turn reflects the desired educational program and practices of the school system. The numbers and types of space the approved educational program required are easily created in a new building. This is not always true in an renovation of an existing building. Physical limitations are always present in such projects. For instance, load-bearing walls may constrain the amount of usable space that can be created. In addition, existing relationships between various components of the building may prevent initiation of new relationships. In these situations, compromise is necessary. The evaluation process must then provide data to enable the educator to decide how much compromise was needed and to what extent modifications in the program were necessary as a result. The compromises made and the circumstances surrounding these could be useful information in future renovation projects.

The critical judgment of a professional educator should be used to determine compliance with the educational specifications. This is the first and most critical evaluation that should be made. The educator/evaluator should go through each area of the building to determine how closely it compares with what was called for in the educational specifications. This evaluation should judge whether or not the right spaces exist in sufficient numbers, if the size and shape are sufficient to support the program, and if the right equipment and accoutrements are readily available. Specific rooms and areas can be easily measured for adequate size. Other observations should reveal if there is sufficient writing space on the walls, the right kind of equipment, proper floor covering, adequate utilities, and whether or not the room is correctly related to surrounding spaces. The resultant report should state precisely what compromises were made in the project in terms of kinds, sizes, and shapes of new space. It should reflect any problems of circulation or supervision, and any deficiencies in elements and equipment.

A narrative evaluation enables some judgments to be made regarding each area, as well as the total physical plant. These judgments can later serve as rationale for corrective action in the case of serious compromises. There is a certain amount of informality to this type of evaluation, but the basis of the evaluation, the educational specifications, is very specific and lends itself to quite accurate measurements.

The most critical time where compromises in the scope of the work could occur in a renovation project is between the time the educational specifications are approved and the beginning of construction. Sometimes budget limitations mandate certain features in the renovation be either reduced or even eliminated. In addition, unforeseen conditions or problems at the building site, not anticipated by the architect or contractor, can cause the cost of the project to increase during construction. When these situations occur, compromises are made if the project is to be kept within the budget. The form these compromises take can oftentimes affect the usefulness of certain spaces.

PROCESS EVALUATION

A renovated building should be perceived by the users as being more useful and supportive of the educational program than it was before. This means that the building should adequately accommodate and even enhance both the learning activities of the students and the teaching activities of the teachers. Whether or not this is the case can be evaluated by simply asking the users about the physical environment of the facility. In addition to this, the persons who participated in the planning process should feel it was a success. A great deal of the success of the project is dependent upon how well the building performs, but the degree and importance of involvement of individuals is also important.

With the emphasis upon site-based management and local control, planning for a renovation should incorporate the needs of the users as they perceive them. Central administration planners can no longer do the planning for persons in the local school building; they cannot tell the staff how their building will be up-graded without their input. Although there may be some overall school system program emphasis and requirements, there should still be a great deal of input from the local site staff regarding needs of the program and students. These needs can be incorporated into the overall renovation project if sufficient care is given to allowing input. The basic factor to be evaluated in this case is how well the persons involved in the planning of the renovation project feel their input was received and used in the project. In addition, the staff need to be asked whether or not they were significantly involved and if the project was effectively planned so that desired results in the building were obtained.

There is no standardized instrument nor even prescribed methodology that can be used for process evaluation of the planning effort for a renovated facility. There are, however, some basic principles of process evaluation that can be used with good results. The underlying concern is whether or not people who were involved in the planning for a renovation project had an opportunity to contribute time and ideas to the planning process and if they feel their contributions were taken seriously and incorporated into the final product. The best way to find this out is by asking those involved. This can be done by questionnaires, surveys, and interviews.

Whatever the method of gathering data, the actual planning process used by the school system should be evaluated. The basic questions to be asked revolve around the method of involvement. Figure 11.1 is a copy of a questionnaire used by one community to evaluate the process of developing a set of educational specifications. Such an instrument could well be modified to be used to gather data for a renovation project. Specific questions concerning special meetings or presentations could be included in the questionnaire. The entire set of questions should reflect the precise process used in planning.

Some school systems use a combination of general meetings, small group meetings, focus groups, and individual consultations with various persons and groups. These data gathering sessions all need to be evaluated to see if they were effective vehicles. The various individuals and groups involved in the planning process—teachers, administrators, central office specialists, students, parents, and community representatives—need to be included. Most planning efforts, however, do not involve that large a number of individuals to require sampling. Data from such evaluations should enable the school board to judge the effectiveness of the planning process, especially if involvement and community input were paramount.

Some school systems videotape the involvement sessions of the various groups and produce a small documentary of the entire planning process. Such a record provides firsthand data on how people were involved in planning the project. A school board could view the tape to gather some information on who was involved and how they were involved. A videotape of planning sessions does not, however, provide significant information on the quality of community input. This can be gathered only by using a survey instrument or personal interview.

An edited version of the videotape could be shown to various community groups to build support for an upcoming project. In situations where a bond issue must be voted before the project is begun, a videotape could be used to promote the bond election. This videotape could also be used for other promotional efforts of the school system.

Princess Anne County Public Schools

1. Do you currently have children enrolled in the public school system?
   Yes ___ No ___
   If so, what school ___
2. Do you feel the community was adequately represented on the planning committee? Yes ___ No ___
   If No, who should have been included in the committee structure?
   ___
3. How many committee planning sessions were you able to attend? ___
4. In general, do you feel these planning efforts were worthwhile?
   Yes ___ No ___
   If No, what reason would you give for them not being worthwhile?
   ___
5. Do you believe the recommendations of the committee will have significant impact on the final decisions concerning the new secondary school?
   Yes ___ No ___
6. Do you feel the facilitators were successful in helping the group reach consensus? Yes ___ No ___
7. Was there sufficient time for the committee to prepare an accurate and complete report? Yes ___ No ___
8. Do you believe the finished school will reflect exactly the recommendations of the planning committee? Yes ___ No ___
   If No, please state why you think it will not ___
   ___
9. Do you believe the completed school facility will be different from existing schools? Yes ___ No ___
10. Were there any constraints which you believe prevented the planning committee from having a more significant input into the educational specifications document? Yes ___ No ___
    If Yes, what were some of those constraints? ___
    ___
11. Did your work and involvement on the planning committee help to clarify or change your opinion about the goals or objectives of the school system?
    Yes ___ No ___
12. What is your gender? Female ___ Male ___
13. What is your age grouping?
    18 – 30 ___
    31 – 45 ___
    46 – 55 ___
    56 – 65 ___
    65 + ___
14. How long have you lived in the school system? ___ Years

Figure 11.1. *Evaluation Instrument for New Schools.*

EVALUATION RESPONSIBILITY

The overall responsibility for seeing that an evaluation takes place rests with the administrator responsible for the care of facilities. In small school systems, this person might be the head of maintenance and operations or the assistant superintendent for business operations. In larger school systems, the person might be the assistant or associate superintendent for school facilities. These are the people who must make certain that an evaluation is completed; otherwise, one will not be done.

There should be one person or office responsible for the conduct of the post-occupancy evaluations of the building. More often than not, the office responsible is that of the maintenance and operations department. This is the most logical office to assume the responsibility of conducting this effort. The evaluation should, however, be in consultation with the instructional department of the school system so that needed data can be gathered. In addition, the first evaluation should be completed by the person who wrote the educational specifications for the renovation project. This is the person most familiar with what is contained in that document and would provide the most accurate evaluation.

Undoubtedly the architect will want to evaluate the completed building to judge the effectiveness of the architectural firm and see how the contractor completed the work. This is, of course, the responsibility of the architectural firm, and the data gathered is more applicable to the work of the architect than the work of the school system. The school system should, however, be interested in the results of the architect's evaluation, if for no other reason than to evaluate the work of the architectural firm.

USE OF EVALUATIVE DATA

The data gathered in the evaluation process can help the school board and administration judge the effectiveness of the school system in managing a planning process. As far as the process evaluation is concerned, the school board can make some judgments on how well the staff worked with community members and how easily they enlist their support for the project. If community involvement was a high priority item, this should be reflected in the data gathered from the people involved.

The school board also needs to find out how well the finished product meets the needs of the educational program. Likewise, it should be judged in terms of being the type of structure needed by that particular faculty to teach effectively. Data concerning the facility should be useful in future renovation projects. If nothing else, the physical problems that occurred during the planning and construction phases should be identified and documented for future use. Undoubtedly, some of the problems encountered in a renovation project could easily be ones that would crop up in other renovation projects. Perhaps knowing these difficulties beforehand would help the architect and administrators overcome these problems or even avoid them in the next project.

EVALUATION PERIOD

The purpose of the evaluation will have great influence on when it should be completed. Obviously, some data can be gathered only at a certain time, such as at the completion of the project. Other data may be gathered at an earlier or later date. Immediately following the completion of the renovation project, the building should be evaluated using the educational specifications as the basis for the evaluation. This evaluation should not only demonstrate how well the building will fit the program, but also identify any of the unforeseen problems that arose during construction. The latter would encompass the problems associated with the lack of as-built architectural drawings of the original building. When such drawings are used, the removal of a wall may well expose an array of utility lines that were not identified on the original architectural drawings. Knowledge of this problem might well assist architect and contractor in another project.

Data on these problems are best gathered immediately after construction. Likewise, data regarding community participation in the planning process is best gathered as soon after the process as possible. This may well be immediately after the planning process and before the renovation project is under construction. Gathering data in a timely fashion is of prime importance for a proper evaluation of both product and process. School system administrators and school boards need to keep this in mind at all times.

REFERENCES

Earthman, G. I. 1992. *Planning Educational Facilities for the Next Century*. Reston, VA: Association of School Business Officials, p. 238.

Macclay, W. R. and G. I. Earthman. 1992. "Post-Occupancy Evaluation of Standley Lake High School," CEFPI, *The Educational Facility Planner*, 30(3):7.

White, E. T. 1992. "Post-Occupancy: A New Component in the Building Delivery Process," CEFPI, *The Educational Facility Planner*, 30(3):4.

CHAPTER 12

Adapting the Building to Educational Trends

INTRODUCTION

IN Chapter 6, an example was given in which a school system completely renovated a sixty-year-old building. Every utility system was replaced or improved, a new roof was applied, and windows were replaced. Even the classrooms and hallways were recarpeted. The cost of the renewal was above 50 percent of the replacement value of the school building, a percentage used by many people as a threshold to determine the feasibility of a renovation. There was, however, no change or improvement made to the building's library. In addition, no substantive or structural improvements had been made to the library space since the building was constructed. For sixty years the library and staff had been housed in a space thought adequate in 1931. To make matters worse, the extensive renovation project insured use of that building for another twenty-five to fifty years. Obviously, library functions and services have changed considerably over the last sixty years, and yet the library space in that building has not qualitatively or quantitatively increased; the library space is inadequate by all current standards.

The above scenario actually happened, it was not an imaginary situation. It is a perfect example of how some people divorce the physical planning activities from the educational planning efforts of the school system. Sometimes physical planning of school systems occurs as an isolated event in the history of the organization and has little relationship to the educational planning of the school system. Planning physical facilities in isolation to the rest of the school system is detrimental to the planning done for educational improvement. This isolation is further carried on in the design phase when an architect has no educational specifications to guide the work. Architects are employed to respond to the well-defined educational program of the school system as enunciated by the staff, but if there are no educational specifications to follow, the architects often suggests designs based upon their own interpretation of what the school system needs. When such a design is implemented in a school building, the educational program is limited to fit the spaces available in the building.

This situation can easily occur in the renovation of an existing building. In the first place, an architectural preliminary or feasibility study is completed before a decision to renovate is made. Although the feasibility or preliminary study is based upon the detailed educational specifications prepared by the school system, the confines of the existing building may preclude developing functional plans that provide the exact kinds of spaces demanded. The end result is that the architect provides spaces believed to fit the educational program, but in reality hinders the flow of students and the placement of groups in adequate spaces or causes the program to change in order to fit the spaces that are available.

Educators can do much to ensure that the design of the building fits the educational program by enunciating quite clearly the specific activities that will take place in the given space. This kind of leadership will go a long way in assuring the best possible teaching/learning space. Detailing what the program is and how it relates to existing spaces and relationships requires considerable attention, especially in a renovation project for an existing building.

Chapter 6 details a process whereby the educators can develop a workable set of educational specifications for a desired program and at the same time significantly involve others in the planning for a renovation project. In this chapter, the effect of educational innovations upon the spaces in a renovated building is discussed with the hope that educators will understand the inextricable relationship between the kinds of activities carried on in an educational program and the types and kinds of spaces that are needed in the building to accommodate the activities.

THE EFFECTS OF THE TEACHING/LEARNING PROCESS

Space should be defined by and designed for the type of activity that will take place. Learning processes and teaching processes occur simultaneously in an instructional space. When the space in which the students and teacher are located supports both their activities and does not hinder them from doing what they are supposed to do, the building enhances the two processes and allows them to proceed effectively.

In renovation, renewal, and modernization projects, the goal and subsequent effort to define proper spaces and relationships is still the same as in planning for a new building. The big difference is that the existing structure presents more limitations to the conceptualization of adequate instructional spaces. The new spaces created in the existing building should provide a better environment for the teaching and learning processes, not just the same kinds of spaces with new paint or wall covering. The creativity of the architect and educational planner is challenged greatly in renovation projects.

One of the main reasons for this difficulty is that existing buildings were constructed for a different kind of program than what is in existence today. The educational program of forty to fifty years ago is not the same as today, even though much of the organization of the school is similar. Many of the school buildings that are approaching fifty years of age were planned for a traditional subject-matter type curriculum organization in the high school and a self-contained grouping in the elementary school. Both of these curricular and instructional models needed buildings that were unique to that type of program and were mostly long structures with double loaded corridors. On the high school level, the buildings were segmented into the various disciplines such as English, social studies, mathematics, science, and foreign language. These disciplines were housed in departmental sections of the buildings. In fact, all of the subject areas of the high school had separate departmental classroom wings or areas. In the elementary school a grade level organizational pattern existed which resulted in buildings that had wings or fingers that contained various grade level classrooms.

Both of these organizational patterns fostered school buildings that contained long halls necessitating load-bearing walls for the corridors. Change in building structure in these types of buildings is extremely difficult because it is hard to visualize new spaces that are not long and narrow.

EDUCATIONAL INNOVATIONS

Educational practice changes constantly and is never in a static state. These changes may be very slight or rather monumental, but are occurring all the time. Changes result from research conducted on how students learn or on more effective teaching methodologies. Again these two processes govern how a school is organized and how the building should be formed and configured. These are the two processes that govern the majority of educational innovations that are current today. Even the organization of the school itself refers to the manner in which teachers group and instruct students.

The three major questions that must be answered in order to have an educational program are the following:

(*1*) What will the students be taught? (Curriculum)
(*2*) How will the students be taught? (Methodology)
(*3*) How will students be grouped for instruction? (Organization)

These are the main questions that must be answered by any school board and administration in order to have any type of educational program. Educators have become so accustomed to having the curriculum identified for them, using the methodology they learned in their course work at the university, and grouping students in pre-determined groups, that they rarely raise these questions or give them serious thought. This is not a condemnation of the vision of educators in the country. Quite the contrary, educators must daily deal with these questions, but not on a fundamental level. The curriculum is rarely scrutinized to determine relevance or purpose for the goals of the schools. New courses are frequently added to the curriculum and different programs become the responsibility of the schools because of outside pressure upon the school system. Almost never is any subject area or program deleted from the curriculum to make way for the new material or because the material is no longer relevant to the goals of the school system. This additive approach to curriculum reform puts more pressure on the teachers to include the new material and still include the regular subjects. The additive approach also dilutes the time devoted to some of the essential parts of the curriculum.

Nevertheless, what is taught—the subject matter of the curriculum—has and should have a tremendous impact upon the number of spaces that are needed and the way the interior of the building is configured. Obviously, the science, vocational education, physical education, and art programs, for example, determine greatly the characteristics of the spaces in which they are taught. Utility services needed in an educational program, the size and kinds of equipment used, and the unique spaces needed to house an educational function all impact the interior of a building. Subject matter has the greatest impact upon building shape when special equipment or technology is needed in the program. When new programs are scheduled to be implemented in a renovated building, the educational planner must know and anticipate the exact needs of the particular program to be implemented.

The question concerning methodology has probably received the most attention with the introduction of various new teaching strategies. But again, there has been little fundamental change over the past four or five decades in the way a teacher is deployed to a specific group of students for instruction. Considerable emphasis is given in current literature to the new role of the teacher from that of a person who imparts knowledge to students to that of one who facilitates the learning process of students. To put that idea into operational terms is rather difficult, because there is not a great deal of difference between the way a good teacher works with students and the way the teacher-facilitator is described in the literature. Naturally, there are very few if any elementary teachers who solely lecture to a class and then expect the students to ingest and regurgitate what was said. Observation in almost any elementary school would reveal the teacher as one who not only facilitates learning, but also guides and instructs students when necessary. Felt (1985) identified six recommendations for improving teaching methods:

(*1*) Increase students' time-on-task
(*2*) Individualize of instruction
(*3*) Provide remediation for students who need it
(*4*) Use variety in teaching techniques and active student involvement
(*5*) Use Socratic Questioning to develop values and understanding
(*6*) Foster academic self-esteem and motivation (Felt, 1985, p.184)

These guidelines serve to help teachers work as facilitators in the education of students. Do these recommendations for teacher activity require different kinds or types of classroom space than the general purpose classroom, or any special equipment? Naturally, none of these recommendations would require any change in the internal structure of the school building or require any particular equipment not found in the schools today to be successfully implemented.

The question concerning the organization of students for effective learning has been addressed only on a cursory basis. Students in the United States have been taught in groups since the founding of the colonies. During the nineteenth century, graded groups developed when large numbers of students in a similar age group arrived at school at the same time. This began early in the urban areas of the country when cities began to experience significant growth. The outcome of this development has been the prototype of a classroom where twenty-five or more students were grouped with one teacher in one classroom. That organizational pattern for students has survived to the present time. Even the latest school buildings to be designed have some method of grouping a pre-determined number of students in a classroom unit. The number of students assigned to a teacher or classroom may have been reduced, but the idea of a certain number of students assigned to a teacher is still quite prevalent. Thus, the total student body is divided by a pre-determined number of students; the resulting product is the number of classrooms or instructional spaces to be included in the school building.

Normally, students are organized into some type of grouping for instructional purposes. Obviously, teaching a group of students is more efficient and cost-effective than teaching individuals. The entire instructional program of the schools in the United States is based upon teaching a group of students. Those few times in history where education was given on an individual basis are no longer possible, if for no other reason than the cost factor. Based upon this, schools need to be planned and designed to accommodate a pre-determined group of students. The resulting buildings will always vaguely represent the school buildings of a century earlier. Only if educators develop an organizational pattern that is different from the standard grouping of a pre-determined number of students and one teacher will there be a need for spaces in a school building radically different from the standardized general purpose classrooms.

Only two significant changes from this universal grouping pattern have occurred in the past century; however, these changes were not universally implemented. The first one was the team-teaching organization espoused by J. Lloyd Trump in the late 1950s (Trump, 1959). This scheme divided a large group of students into various sized groups for different kinds of instruction throughout the day. This resulted in a school building with a number of different sized instructional spaces—large, medium, and small groups—as well as individual study spaces. This organizational pattern is no longer employed to any extent in this country today; however, there are some organizational plans, such as the Copernican Plan, for restructuring high schools that resemble the so-called Trump Plan (Carroll, 1989).

The other variation in grouping students for instruction was the open space education plan, which was employed in many elementary schools and unsuccessfully in some secondary schools in the 1960s (Graves, 1993). The open education or open classroom teaching strategy and the open space classroom teaching strategy are often thought of as being the same. Open education is based upon the philosophy of the British Primary School model (Blitz, 1973). The open space classrooms in some cases incorporated the open education ideas and methods, but the main characteristic was the open area in the school where a number of students were housed for instruction. The idea behind this grouping pattern was that a large group of elementary students would be under the instructional responsibility of a group or team of teachers who planned cooperatively for the instruction of the entire group. The large group was subdivided into various sized groupings for instructional purposes. The student composition in the small groups changed according to their learning needs which could be on a weekly or monthly basis depending upon the progress of the student.

Both organizational plans have been abandoned in common practice throughout the country although vestiges of these philosophies and organizational strategies can be found in various school systems. The buildings that were designed for open space education, however, still exist. The internal structure of these buildings have been modified over time to reflect more current thinking regarding the grouping of students. The open space classrooms have been closed to form self-contained spaces in which groups of students and one teacher work. The high schools that were designed to accommodate the variable group instructional methodology have been converted to regular-sized classroom spaces to accommodate conventional high school instructional groups of students. These modifications have occurred as the educational program has changed over the years. This type of internal structural change within a building to reflect program change will also need to happen when renovation or renewal of existing buildings takes place in the future.

The answers to the three questions posed earlier in the chapter do have an impact upon the building; each of the components of the school operation identified in the questions serve to determine how the internal structure of the school building is configured. The curriculum does demand certain types of spaces because of the subject matter being taught and the equipment used in the teaching and learning processes. The manner in which students are taught, or the methodology used, does require certain kinds and types of instructional spaces, and, in addition, the way students are grouped has an obvious impact upon how the instructional spaces are designed. Therefore, any change in the curriculum, methodology, or organization of a school program must be reflected in how an existing school is renovated to accommodate these changes.

Many of the educational innovations and reform measures that are espoused in current literature and practiced in the schools take place within the confines of the group structure normally found in a general purpose classroom. These teaching strategies do not need any special space or equipment other than what is found in the regular classroom spaces of the school building, or if special equipment is utilized by either the teacher or student, it can easily be located in the normal classroom.

Walacavage (1993) identified several significant educational innovations in discussing their effect upon buildings:

- interdisciplinary or integrated curriculum
- thematic units – curriculum integration
- team teaching
- cooperative or collaborative learning
- outcome based education (OBE)
- non-graded student grouping
- real life learning
- essential schools – schools-within-schools
- student video productions
- new areas of instruction: inquiry/expression; history/philosophy; science/math; literature/fine arts
- interest/learning centers
- technology

Added to that list could be the inclusion/immersion model for special education, problem-based learning, peer teaching, group learning, tech-prep programs, assertive discipline, and a host of other innovations or improvements that are currently circulating in the field of education. Many of these suggested innovations are duplicative in practice and different in name only, and they deal more with the philosophy of learning and teaching than with any well-defined, unique theory of learning that is different from that found across the country in any good school. Only a few of the innovations above would need special spaces; for the most part, the techniques listed above could be initiated within the structure of existing buildings. The practices that might possibly need special space or equipment would be

- interdisciplinary or integrated curriculum
- team teaching
- student video productions
- Interest/Learning Centers

- inclusion/immersion model
- technology
- professionalization of teachers
- schools-within-schools or house plan organization

Technology and student video production would definitely have an impact upon the type and kinds of spaces needed for implementation, as well as the need for specialized equipment. Other technological innovations might need different kinds of spaces than are available in existing school buildings, unless the building was previously designed for them. Interdisciplinary or integrated curriculum models often include teachers working in a team configuration. These two innovations seem to work together in most applications. For instance, in a high school, part of the building could be devoted to an interdisciplinary team of teachers who would be responsible for the instruction of a given large group of students. The students would be assigned to classroom groups with a team of teachers. The team would work as a single unit in organizing their schedules to teach English, social studies, mathematics, foreign language, and in some situations even science to one segment of the student population. This type of teaching strategy would also lend itself to some form of block scheduling in which these students would be rostered successively over four or five contiguous periods of study. By doing this, these same students would be taught by one team of teachers and would not have to leave the group of classrooms assigned to this team for the major part of the day. Such a schedule and curricular approach would best be implemented in a building that would have a block of classrooms grouped in one part of the building in such a way that there would not be a great deal of student movement in the main hall getting from one classroom to another. Of course, a modified version of this curricular and scheduling plan could be implemented in a building that was originally designed for the traditional subject-matter instructional plan, but the implementation of the plan would be compromised because of the inappropriate facilities, and the real benefits of the scheme might be lost or greatly reduced. Renovation of an existing building for an educational program that incorporated these curricular and scheduling innovations would require considerable planning and design work to create the desired kinds of spaces from the existing, traditional, double-loaded corridor areas.

Some school systems have become interested in developing an organizational scheme on the secondary school level that would permit the division of the student body into smaller units. This concept is sometimes referred to as the house plan or a school-within-a-school organization. Basically, in this plan students are grouped into small schools or houses within the total school population; a high school of 1,200 students might be divided into four units or houses of 300 students each. This unit or house would then be located in a section of the building especially designed to accommodate instruction in four or five different subject areas. The configuration of the instructional spaces or classrooms used in this plan would be centered around certain support facilities, and the whole section of the building designed to allow this group of students to study and receive instruction. The space would be defined in such a way that both teachers and students would constitute a minor school within the total secondary school.

There seems to be little operational difference between the idea of a house plan and the school-within-a-school. Both plans are used to organize the student body into smaller groups for the purpose of instruction. The school-within-a-school concept may be the more comprehensive in that all of the educational programs and services are physically located within the area where the students receive instruction. The guidance and administrative functions as well as the instructional program for at least five basic subject areas, are located within the smaller school organization under this concept. The house plan can be as comprehensive as the school-within-a-school idea, if so organized; however, the house plan can also be used where only one or two subject matter areas of the curriculum are desired, if desired. A school system could organize a house where English and social studies are taught, for example. As is the case with so many educational organizational plans, the concept is defined more by local application in the school system than anything else. An example of a comprehensive house plan is illustrated in Figure 12.1. This space relationship diagram was developed to describe the way facilities might be arranged in a new school building. In this plan, instruction in English, social studies, foreign language, special education, mathematics, and science would be provided for a small unit of students in this one house; students would be scheduled for four or five periods per day without leaving the house. This arrangement eliminates considerable student movement throughout the total building. More importantly, the teachers assigned to this house can plan cooperatively for the student group and practice some interdisciplinary teaching.

Creating such a house or school-within-a-school space might be

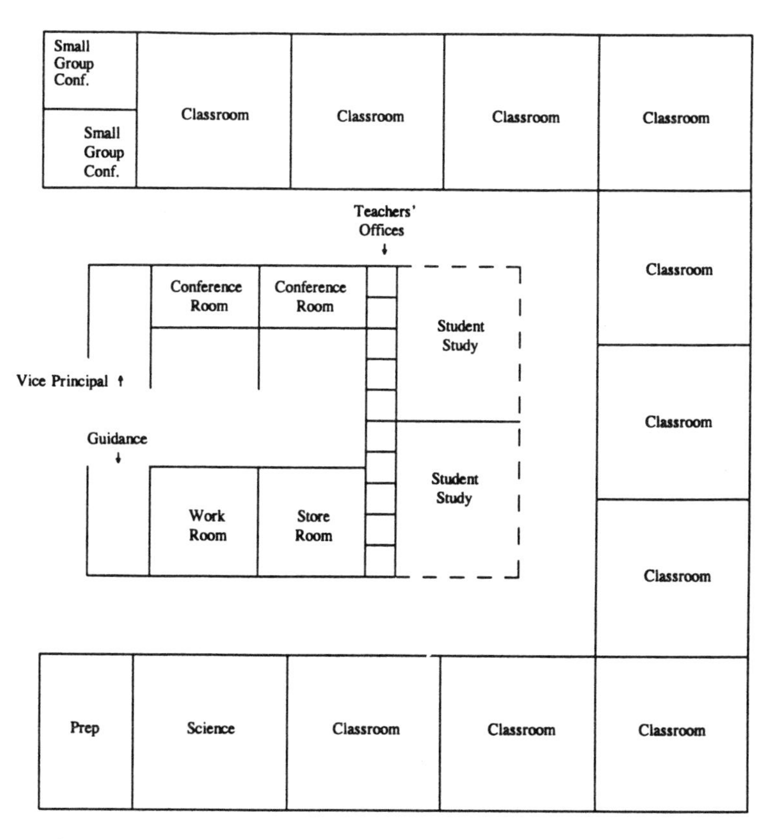

Figure 12.1. *The House Plan (Drawing Designed by Gorge E. Ortiz).*

difficult in a renovation or renewal project in an existing building; however, the task would not be impossible. Considerable planning and design work is needed to create such a reorganization of space. It might be necessary to construct an addition as well as seriously alter the interior space of an existing building to achieve the kind of environment needed to implement this organizational practice.

"Interest/learning center" is a term used to describe an area of the classroom in which various materials, supplies, equipment, and exhibits are contained. The idea behind these centers is that students work independently in these interest areas or centers by using the materials and supplies, manipulating the equipment, and/or viewing the exhibits to gather information to help solve a problem. These centers could be devoted to a discipline such as science, reading, or mathematics, or to topics such as transportation, housing, or personal improvement. Students would discover or conceptualize problems at the center, and by using the material, equipment, or exhibits, solve them. These centers need sufficient space to accommodate several students at one time, plus some tables for the materials, equipment, and exhibits. Obviously, a large classroom would be needed to adequately accommodate several such centers, but on the other hand, teachers in small classrooms can still implement the concept using fewer centers. In renovating an existing building, the educational planner should be aware of the size of classrooms needed, not only to house a certain number of students, but also to implement such educational innovations adequately. This may result in larger-sized classrooms than are currently in existence in the building.

The professionalization of teachers usually means, in educational parlance, the provision of an office or separate individual work space for the teacher. Teachers' offices have been provided in new buildings for quite some time; however, in many school systems across the country, this is an innovation. It is a very practical innovation; not only does the teacher get an appropriate work space, but the classrooms can be used more efficiently than by assigning a teacher to one classroom for the entire school day. In renovating or modernizing an existing building, the educational planner should anticipate this need and make provisions for teacher offices. This may mean that present classroom space will have to be converted for the teacher planning function, which will thereby reduce the total student capacity of the building. The benefits to providing teachers with offices, however, is that better planning on the part of the teacher could result which will then, in turn, improve the instructional program.

In addition to these innovative practices, there have been major efforts to restructure the high school. Two educators have contributed very thoughtful discussions about how the high school should be changed to reflect the needs of today. Sizer (1985, 1992) worked with a group of high schools to promote changes in their program, based upon research findings from *A Study of High Schools,* sponsored by the National Association of Secondary School Principals and the National Association of Independent Schools. These schools formed a ''Coalition of Essential Schools'' to assist each other. The Coalition formed nine principles which serve to differentiate them from most other schools, suggesting a concerted effort for restructuring:

(*1*) The school should focus on helping adolescents learn to use their minds well.

(*2*) The school's goals should be simple: each student should master a number of essential skills and be competent in certain areas of knowledge.

(*3*) The school's goals should apply to all students, but the means to these goals will vary as these students themselves vary.

(*4*) Teaching and learning should be personalized to the maximum feasible extent.

(*5*) The governing metaphor of the school should be student as worker, rather than the more familiar metaphor of teacher as deliverer of instructional services.

(*6*) Students embarking on secondary school studies are those who show competence in language and elementary mathematics.

(*7*) The tone of the school should explicitly and self-consciously stress the value of unanxious [sic] expectations, of trust, and of decency.

(*8*) The principal and teachers should perceive of themselves first as generalists and next as specialists.

(*9*) Administrative and budget targets should include substantial time for collective planning by teachers, competitive salaries for staff, and an ultimate per pupil cost not more than 10 percent higher than that at traditional schools. (Sizer, 1992, p. 207)

Most of the schools in the Coalition are in the early stages of restructuring and can report very little substantive data, yet these schools do report, according to Sizer (1992), improved student academic performance, attendance, morale, and admission to colleges. When these nine principles are viewed as to their possible impact upon the physical facilities of the school, it is difficult to say what exact changes were required to implement them. Principle #4 states that teaching should be personalized to the maximum feasible extent and that the teacher should have direct responsibility for no more than eighty students. This is down from the normal 125 students that high school teachers see each day and would mean a reduction in 45 students or the equivalent of at least two sections. Implementation of this principle would mean either that there are fewer students in each class or that the teacher would teach fewer periods each day, resulting in fewer students being served by this teacher. This principle could have an impact upon a school building in that the overall utilization capacity might be reduced. Inasmuch as most schools are used at only an 85 percent rate, it would seem possible to incorporate this reduced pupil/teacher ratio without necessarily reducing the size of the student body that could be housed in the building. Implementation of the remainder of the principles would require very little, if any, change in existing facilities.

TECHNOLOGY IN EDUCATION

One of the most important concerns in educational reform and restructuring efforts is how the use of technology can support implementation of various teaching strategies or programs. Thoughtful educators and experts in the field of technology have joined to develop some programs that incorporate the best use of the various elements of technology improving the educational program throughout the country.

Unfortunately, some educators equate the word "technology" to the use of computers, but the idea of applying technological assistance to the process of teaching/learning goes beyond that. Generally speaking, technological assistance refers to several of the many ways of electronically making information available to the teacher and student. Some educators refer to integrated learning systems (ILS) as the definition of the use of technology in education (Knirk, 1993). An integrated learning system involves the use of hardware and software in a coordinated effort to provide a total learning environment for the student. This definition would include, but not be limited to, such devices as personal computers, video camera recorders and players (VCRs), televisions, CD-Roms, tape players, laser disks, satellite dishes, record players, and even telephone communication devices (Ross and Stewart, 1993).

There are many innovations that require the use of a computer terminal, whether it is a free-standing personal computer or a computer that is networked to other data sources. The keyboard and monitor of a computer are essential to many of the innovative programs in use today. One such innovation is an integrated learning system where the computer serves as the basis for obtaining information for the student through a number of different sources and modes, and provides an accounting system for student self-progress reports (Knirk, 1993). As a result, teachers need to have computer stations in every teaching area of the school. The challenge for the educational planner in a renovation project is to provide sufficient additional space in each classroom for computers and make provisions for the necessary wiring. This could well mean that a standard, general purpose classroom would be larger in size than what is currently specified now in order to accommodate the increase in numbers of computers.

The use of personal computers is probably the most widespread application of technology, or at least educators seem to imply that it is. It certainly is one of the most exciting applications and perhaps the most interesting to the user. The use of both internal and public television signals in the schools, however, has been in use longer and may have more universal impact. The use of computers and television signals probably constitutes the majority of the applications of technology to education in the schools today, but someday even more advanced technology will be implemented in every school at a sophisticated level.

Regardless of the type of technological assistance that is being employed, the educational planner must describe the use of the device. The best way to do this is to ask the important questions that will provide the architect with sufficient data to design the distribution system. The following planning guidelines can be used to help answer these questions.

(*1*) Determine the specific requirements for each system. Generate a short description of the function needed.

(*2*) List the features important to the operation of the program.

(*3*) Indicate the points of system control.

(*4*) Identify the individuals who will have access to and use of the equipment.

(*5*) Determine the growth potential of the various systems.

By answering these criteria the appropriate wiring and equipment system can be developed for proper use, thereby supporting the educational program in the manner required.

In planning a new school building the educational planner can specify the technology needs and the architect can design appropriate raceways, ducts, and channels to accommodate the wiring needs of any and all systems. Because this portion of the design work is done during the design process of the entire building, few problems are encountered in providing appropriate entry and termination points and adequate raceways for wiring a new building. Such is not necessarily the case in renovating or renewing an existing building. The placement of wiring in an older building requires considerable thought and planning. Most buildings over thirty years old were constructed long before technology was considered an important installation. Load-bearing walls that extend to the roof must be penetrated in order for the wiring to be run to certain points in the building. Many architects state that the use of a drop ceiling in an older building is the best way to distribute the wiring system throughout these structures. In buildings that have been built on a concrete slab, it is are almost impossible to run wiring in the flooring unless channels are cut into the concrete. Consequently, the use of the plenum above the ceiling to provide raceways is one of the best ways to distribute wire this type of building.

In renovating an existing building the electrical service must be improved to accommodate the increased lighting needs and also the increased use of electrical equipment, especially computers. Some engineers suggest the electrical service for computers be put on a separate circuit for better service (Geiger, 1993). In this manner the voltage of the circuits serving the computer equipment is more stable, and a Transient Voltage Spike Suppressor (TVSS) can be provided at the service location and at panelboards serving voltage sensitive loads. The TVSS reduces electrical surges, which are detrimental to computer equipment and can damage data files.

Two methods for distributing electrical service to banks of computers have been suggested. In a renovation or renewal project engineers have been successful in developing a wall-mounted system for running wiring around the perimeter of the classroom and thus allowing electrical outlets to be installed wherever needed. Another method of distributing electrical service to equipment has been the use of electrical poles that carry the wiring through a ceiling channel and down through the pole which contains electrical outlets. Both methods have been successfully implemented in renovated space.

As the availability of computers increases, more schools will begin to implement some type of integrated learning system to allow for students to formulate individual learning packages (Knirk, 1993). The basis of this system is the personal computer which provides the access to various software and learning systems. This innovative practice can be very simple or it can be developed to a high degree of sophistication. In planning the space for any integrated learning system, regardless of what the components may be, there are many factors the educational planner must consider:

(*1*) Lighting
(*2*) Furniture
(*3*) Wiring
(*4*) Space
(*5*) Security
(*6*) Material storage

(*7*) Materials accessibility
(*8*) Ambient noise and sound control
(*9*) Temperature control
(*10*) The relevant codes and laws pertaining to safety, fire, and student density (Knirk, 1992, p. 13)

Relevant specifications to describe these factors need to be written by the educational planner so that the architect can then design the proper space. Each of these factors relate to certain determined measurements such as the amount of ambient light needed for a computer space; the type, number, and kind of wiring needed for the specific technology employed; temperature levels and limits; tolerated decibel levels; required square footage; and legal requirements. The responsibility of the educational planner in this matter is to describe the educational activity that will take place, the materials and equipment that will be used during these activities, and the relationships to be observed between building components. The architect uses this information during design of the space and classroom accoutrements.

The type of educational program to be implemented in a building needs to be properly housed in spaces that allow students and teachers to engage in pertinent activities. In planning and designing a new building, physical constraints to this should be minimized. In fact, a new building cannot only properly house the existing program, but usually sufficient flexibility is designed into the new structure to allow the building to be converted, altered, and changed to meet new program demands. This is not necessarily so in older buildings. When older structures are renovated or renewed, there may be considerable difficulty in obtaining the right number and kinds of spaces that an educational program will need. The primary reason for such difficulty is the existing physical structure of the building, which in so many cases contains physical barriers and limitations.

Much of the trends for student populations throughout the country suggests a continued growth pattern. This means a continued need for more school space to house the expanding population. In addition, America has a tremendous investment in the number of school buildings owned and operated by local school systems. All of this suggests a continued use of existing buildings. A great number of school buildings will soon reach the age of fifty years and will need considerable attention. With appropriate planning, these buildings could serve the student population into the next century.

REFERENCES

Blitz, B. 1973. *The Open Classroom: Making It Work.* Boston: Allyn and Bacon, p. 262.

Boyer, E. L. 1983. "High School: An Agenda for Action," Reprint of Chapter 18, *High School,* New York: Harper and Row Publishers, Inc.

Carroll, J. M. 1989. *The Copernican Plan: Restructuring the American High School.* Andover, MA: The Regional Laboratory for Educational Improvement of the Northeast and Islands, p. 103.

Felt, M. C. 1985. *Improving Our Schools.* Newton, MA: Educational Development Center, Inc., p. 224.

Graves, B. E. 1993. *School Ways: The Planning and Design of America's Schools.* NY: McGraw-Hill, Inc., p. 238.

Geiger, C. H. 1993. "Electrical and Communications Systems for Schools." Presentation at Conference, Building Schools to Meet Changing Needs, Madison: University of Wisconsin.

Knirk, F. G. 1993. "Facility Requirements for Integrated Learning Systems," *The Educational Facility Planner,* Dublin, Ohio: The Council of Educational Facility Planners, International, 31(3):13–18.

Ross, T. W. and G. K. Stewart. 1993. "Facility Planning for Technology Implementation," *The Educational Facility Planner,* Dublin, OH: The Council of Educational Facility Planners, International, 31(3):9–12.

Sizer, T. R. 1985. *Horace's Compromise: The Dilemma of the American High School.* Boston, MA: Houghton Mifflin Company, p. 255.

Sizer, T. R. 1992. *Horace's School: Redesigning the American High School.* Boston, MA: Houghton Mifflin Company, p. 238.

Trump, J. L. 1959. *Images of the Future.* Urbana, IL: Commission on the Experimental Study of the Utilization of the Staff in the Secondary School, p. 46.

Walacavage, C. 1993. "Facility Implications of New Teaching Methodologies of the 1980s and 1990s: A Bibliographic Essay," Unpublished paper. Fairfax, VA: Ingraham Planning Associates, p. 1.

Madison County High School Renovation and Renewal

SCHOOL DESCRIPTION

MADISON County encompasses a suburban area of a major city and has a population that exceeds many cities. This unincorporated county has many sub-developments which produce a sizable student population. There are eight high schools in the county, one of which is Madison County High School. The Madison County High School was constructed in 1968 and is situated on a site containing forty-four acres in the northern part of the county. The school is in a residential area, and because of shifts of population in the general area, the attendance zone has been changed several times in the twenty-five years the school has been in operation. The original building was constructed for $11,000,000. The cost of the site, equipment, and fees raised the total cost of the high school by another $1,400,000.

The original school capacity was 2,200 students, but the enrollment at the time of the renovation was 1,800, reflecting some of the shifting population. Prior to the renovation, the professional staff numbered 168, including the principal and three assistant principals.

RENOVATION/RENEWAL PROJECT

The Madison County Public Schools has a program of renewing or modernizing schools when the building reach twenty to twenty-five years old. The school system's renewal program identifies all school buildings in the county the fall within that age group each year. These buildings are then selected for renewal. The intent of the program is to bring all school buildings up to the standard of the most recently constructed building. In this way, the county can insure some type of equity in educational facilities between the various sections of the county. The renewal program also identifies the type and extent of work that is to be done in the renewal/renovation process. A copy of the general scope of work is contained in Appendix B. In addition to the general scope of work, each school building is evaluated to determine other segments of the renewal/renovation. In the case of the Madison County High School building, additions were scheduled because of program needs.

The Madison County High School building was identified for funding during the 1992–93 school year to the extent of $11,000,000. Replacement cost of this high school was estimated at $21,000,000 plus equipment and fees, or a total of $23,500,000. This did not include the cost of a new site. Inasmuch as the school system needed to have a high school in the area to accommodate the student population and to address the facilities equity issue, the decision was made to renovate/renew the building.

The general scope of work included items for the four major systems of the building–architectural/structural, mechanical, plumbing, and electrical–plus the site. The budgeted amount of the renovation was distributed as follows:

- $9,000,000–construction contract which included the renovation of the existing building and site
- $350,000–furniture and movable equipment
- $1,650,000–an addition to the building of 10,000 square feet of new construction

In addition to the items contained in the general scope of work, specific items needed attention to improve the school and provide the types of spaces a modern educational program requires:

- *Hall congestion*–Part of the library was used for circulation in the front hall. The library was an open space on one side to permit students to circulate from one part of the building to another. To prevent loss of books, a security system was installed. This security system slowed student traffic and considerable congestion occurred before and after school, as well as during every change of classes throughout the day. A better definition of the circulation pattern was needed to prevent congestion.
- *Library*–The open space plan of the library and subsequent security system not only caused congestion, but also resulted in

considerable disruption in a traditionally quiet area. What was need was to have a secure area for the library function and at the same time permit access to the library holdings. Also, the existing library was not capable of handling the improvements in technology in the access and use of information.

- *Lecture hall*—The large group lecture hall was simply two classes joined together. The floor was flat and had four parallel walls. There were electrical service outlets on only two walls, the front and back. Lighting was fixed and of poor quality. Movable student arm chair desks were in use the room was not very functional for large group lectures.
- *Classroom space*—Over the years, many classrooms had been converted to computer labs. This reduced the capacity of the school sufficiently to cause the school staff concern in light of recent community growth. Additional general purpose classroom space was needed to accommodate the growth of the student population and increase in computer labs.
- *Technology*—The school building was designed during a period of time when technology was not a great concern. As a result, the building lacked sufficient electrical power and outlets to accommodate the increase in equipment. In addition, there was a lack of visual and audio communication between the classrooms and various other areas, such as the library, within the building, and between other schools in the county. The cooling system was incapable of keeping the computer laboratories at a workable and/or comfortable temperature level.
- *Parking*—Because of the growth in automobile usage by students and teachers over the years, the existing parking area became overcrowded and inadequate and needed expansion.

Beside these major items, the total scope of the project included some requests from the staff of the school:

- *Guidance*—more offices and conference rooms
- *Music*—additional space for the orchestra program
- *Drama*—better lighting in theater, dressing rooms
- *Business*—additional labs
- *Physical Education*—new gymnasium and supporting facilities

These requests were evaluated for need in light of limited resources. The request of the guidance staff, music department, drama department, and physical education department were included in the renovation project. Some of the requests were included in the new construction; other needs were incorporated in the renovation of the existing space. The following items were included in the square footage that was added to the new building:

- *Open court infill*—A two-story addition was constructed in one of the open courtyards. This addition housed a lecture hall and nine new instructional areas—Four classrooms, two mathematics computer labs, one business computer lab, and two special education classrooms.
- *Music storage*—An area of 1,200 square feet was added to the building for instrument and uniform storage.
- *Auditorium lobby extension*—The music storage addition permitted the lobby of the auditorium to be expanded.
- *Arcade infills*—There were two arcades or breezeways in the academic portion of the building. These were enclosed to form lobbies. Additional offices and storage areas were also gained through this enclosure.

RENOVATION/RENEWAL RESULTS

The architects worked with the staff of the high school and the central office in designing the new spaces and the renovation of the existing space. The results of the design phase were put out for bid and a contract was awarded to a successful bidder who was a local contractor.

In a complete renovation project, the Madison County Public Schools allows renovation work by a contractor while school is in session. Some school systems are able to move the entire student body to a different building for the time of the renovation project, but in this case the educational program for the students at the high school was not interrupted. The county obtained five temporary classrooms and placed them on the site of the high school. The plan was that five classes would be moved out of the building and into the temporary classrooms while work was being done on vacated classrooms. When the contractor was finished with those five classrooms, a different five classrooms would be vacated and moved to the temporary classroom units. In the case of Madison County High School, the social studies team of teachers volunteered to stay in the temporary classrooms for the entire period of the renovation project. The rotation of the vacant classroom still continued with various subject departments moving out of their classrooms into finished classrooms and then back into the original classrooms. This rotation continued for the entire two years of the renovation project.

What was completed during the renovation and new construction was the following:

- *Hall congestion*—A new front hallway was constructed to allow students to go from the academic units to the administrative suite without going through the library.
- *Library*—The existing library was enclosed and expanded into the multi-purpose room which enlarged the area for the library function. The library now has a central entrance with a new circulation desk. An electronic classroom was created and new equipment installed.
- *Technology*—A new and increased electrical service to the building was installed—existing wiring was replaced with new wiring. Electrical wall molding was installed in almost every instructional area to provide electrical and telecommunication service. Electrical poles were used in many classrooms and computer labs to bring electrical service where needed.

  Special four pipe heating and cooling was installed in all computer sites to insure even temperature in those areas.

  The school was equipped with a telecommunication infrastructure which included fiber optic wiring. Two outlets of four pair shielded twisted pair ran from the fiber optic backbone to each classroom unit.
- *Open court infill*—The courtyard infill provided the additional classrooms and a lecture hall seating 200 students. The lecture hall was equipped with sophisticated sound and telecommunication equipment to become a top flight lecture area.
- *Parking*—The parking area was resurfaced and different parking widths used to increase the parking by 100 additional spaces.

RENOVATION PROBLEMS

As in every construction project, the renovation/renewal project of Madison County High School generated some problems for the school staff. Classes were interrupted daily for any number of reasons. Several times there was an interruption of electrical service to a wing of the building or the entire building. The local fire marshal became a frequent visitor to the school for either problems with the construction operation or false alarms. The movement of classes and teachers from classroom to classroom to vacate their rooms caused considerable confusion; however the educational program was not seriously interrupted during the two-year period of the renovation project.

PROJECT OUTCOME

The first question to be raised about a renovation/renewal project concerns the success of the efforts. Was the resultant school facility what the educators wanted and needed? Does the facility permit the implementation of an educational program equal to that of the newest high school building? The answers to both questions in the case of the Madison County High School is an unequivocal affirmation.

The high school building does contain the numbers and types of educational spaces a modern high school needs to function effectively. The building is presently able to handle the technology requirements the county educators perceive as being needed in the next few years. Further, the building has been expanded in those areas that were constrained.

The renovated Madison County High School will be able to serve the youth of the county for another twenty-five years in an effective manner, and the project cost less than constructing a new building on the existing site. Although the financial consideration entered the decision making process, the fact that the building was in good condition at the time of renovation and that there was a need for a school building in this area were contributing factors in deciding to renovate the building.

SCHOOL PLANS

The following pages contain line drawings of the school before and after renovation and addition. Drawings A and B are the floor plans of the school before renovation. Drawings C and D are the floor plans after the renovation project was completed.

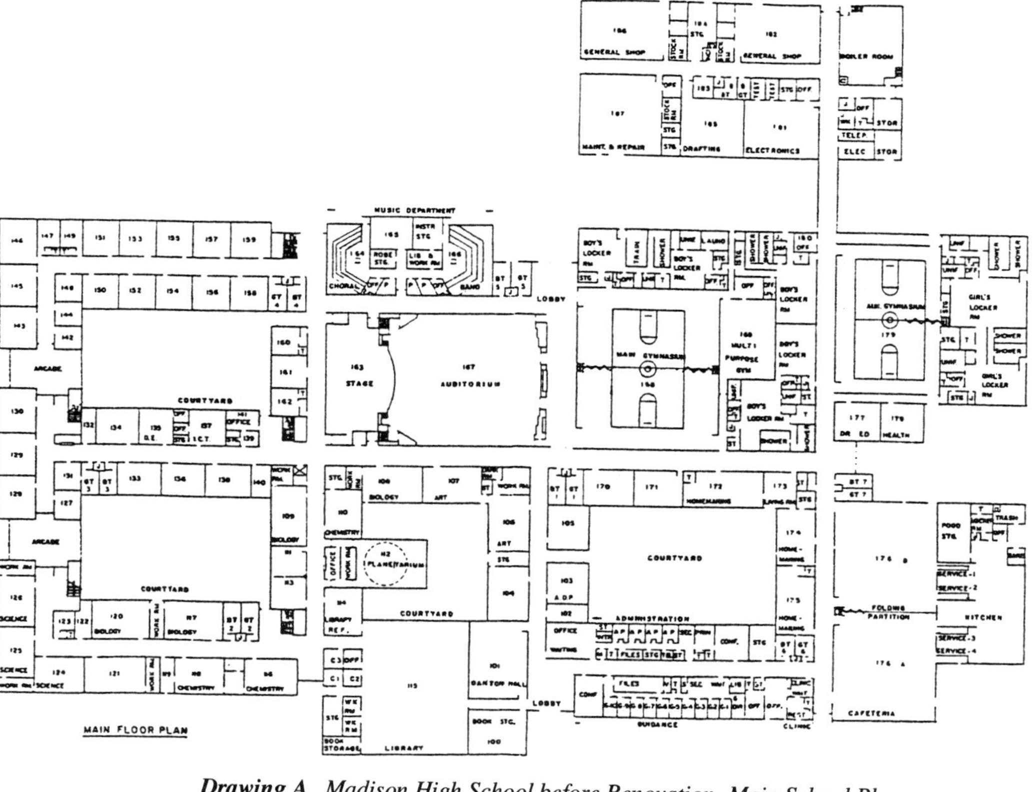

Drawing A. *Madison High School before Renovation, Main School Plan.*

Drawing B. *Madison High School before Renovation, Upper Floor Plan.*

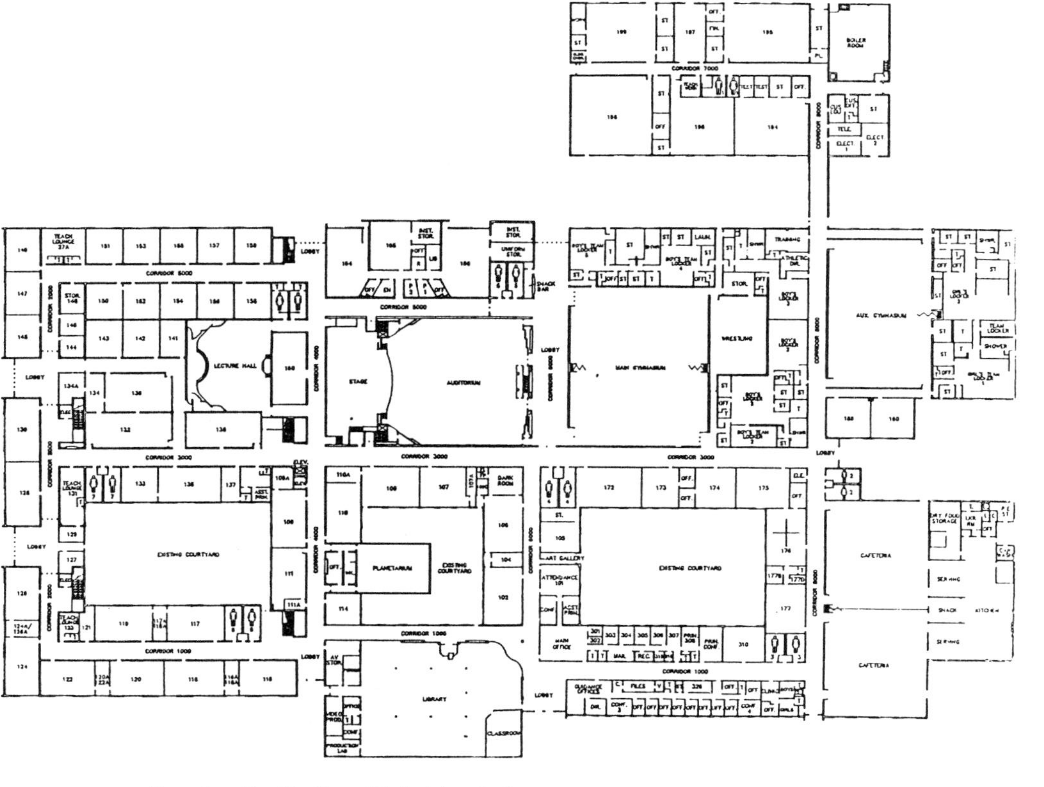

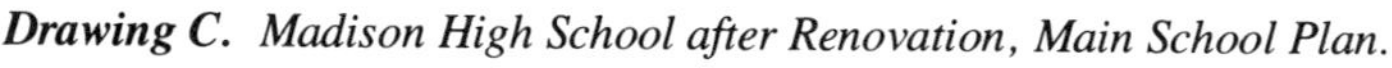

Drawing C. *Madison High School after Renovation, Main School Plan.*

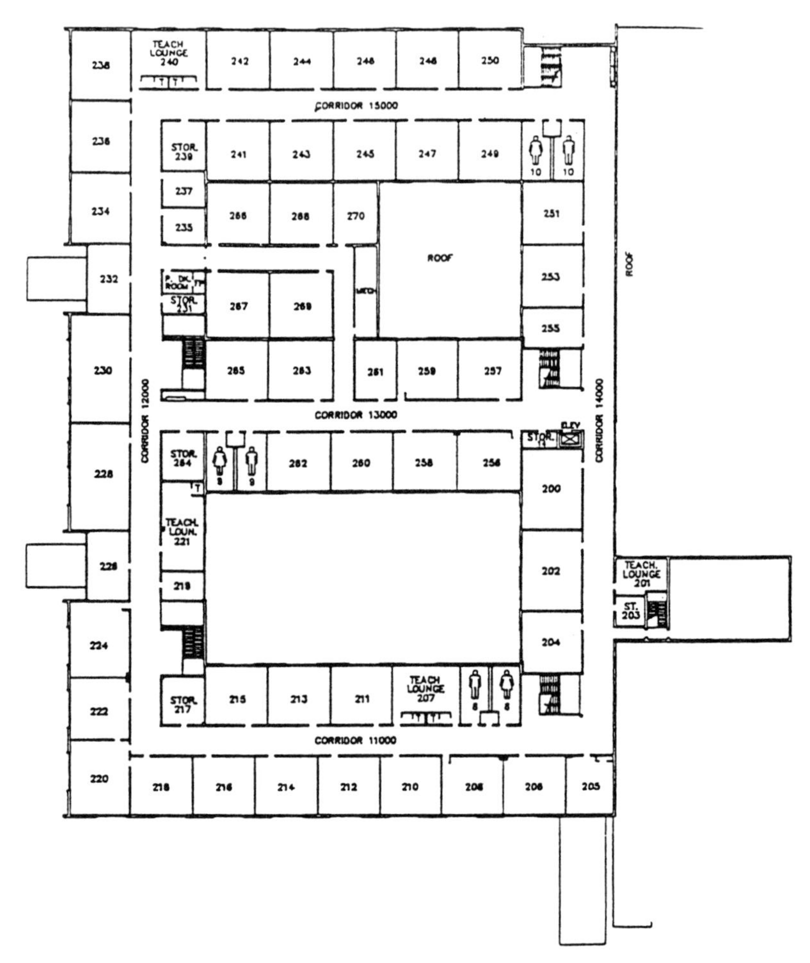

Drawing D. *Madison High School after Renovation, Upper Floor Plan.*

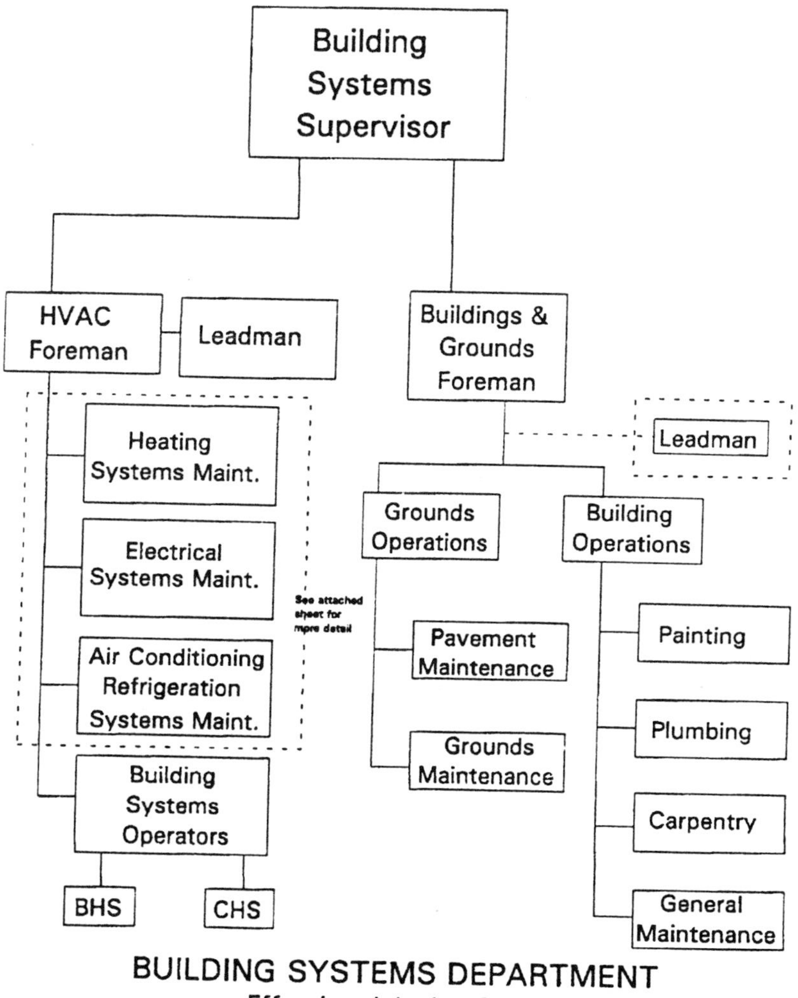

BUILDING SYSTEMS DEPARTMENT
Effective July 1, 1991

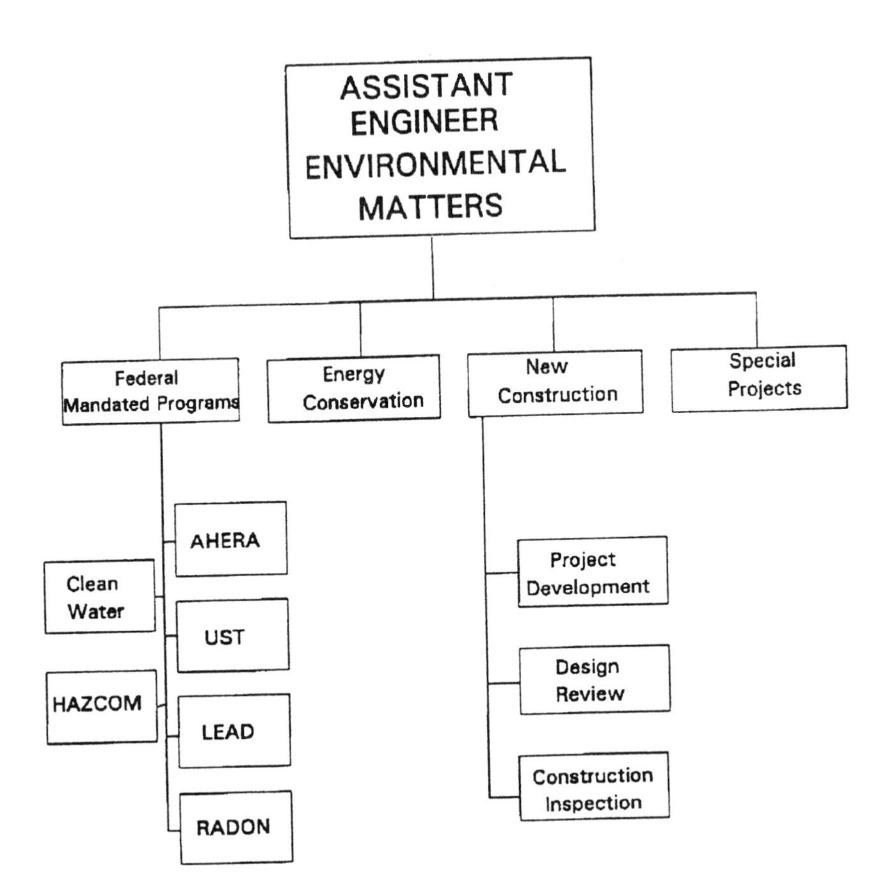

ASSISTANT ENGINEER
Functional Organization

General Scope of Work – Fairfax County Public Schools

GENERAL SCOPE OF WORK FOR ELEMENTARY SCHOOL RENEWAL AND ADDITION

General

(*1*) Renew, upgrade existing facilities such as roof, mechanical, and electrical systems to provide a twenty-year life expectancy.

(*2*) Meet with principal and staff for their input and wish list within budget; coordinate items listed by maintenance.

(*3*) Develop a detailed scope of work that meets defined budget for review by Design and Construction.

Site

(*1*) Check all asphalt paving conditions; repair, cap where required.

(*2*) Check all concrete walks, curb, and gutter conditions, repair where required.

(*3*) Provide handicapped curb cuts.

(*4*) Evaluate existing parking conditions; expand parking if additional spaces are deemed necessary.

(*5*) Evaluate site lighting and replace/upgrade fixtures where required.

Architectural

(*1*) New construction will be required to provide additional support space. New construction may be required at main office, media center, cafeteria, and for School Age Child Care (SACC). Verify that kindergarten rooms meet S.F. requirements.

(*2*) Meet with Department of Energy Management and Fire Marshal to determine extent of fire alarm system, sprinkler, fire doors, stairway enclosures, and fire separations.

(*3*) Provide handicap facilities throughout, including interior and exterior ramps, elevator (where applicable), handicapped toilet stalls, handicapped, EWC, etc.

(*4*) Provide extra storage if possible.

(*5*) Renovate library and expand if necessary.

(*6*) Renovate main office and expand if necessary; main office must have visual control of main entrance from reception area.

(*7*) Provide termite control for any new construction.

(*8*) Increase size of mail box in main office for additional teachers.

(*9*) Renovate/replace existing sink and base cabinet units in classroom.

(*10*) Check condition of existing roof (see roof report). Re-roof if required. Provide additional roof drains where ponding exists.

(*11*) Increase building envelope insulation for energy conservation, i.e., insulation and "Insulcrete" over glass block.

(*12*) Replace, refinish exterior and interior door; provide new panic hardware on all doors with same (rim device only); and weatherstrip all exterior doors.

(*13*) Provide security in all exterior doors, and administration, media, kitchen, dry food storage, exterior storage, and computer rooms.

(*14*) Replace all interior door glass side lights, etc., with 3/16″ laminated glass or 1/8″ tempered glass.

(*15*) Replace all exterior windows with insulated glass, aluminum frame windows.

(*16*) Repaint the entire building's interior and exterior. Paint site items such as flag poles, light poles, fencing, out-buildings, playground equipment, etc.

(*17*) Provide new acoustical tile ceilings throughout:
- rock face tile—corridors, locker rooms, toilets
- smooth vinyl surface—kitchen
- standard acoustical tile—entire building except as noted above

Remove all class "C" 12″ × 12″ ceiling tile, wood furring, Kraft-paper faced fiberglass insulation; replace insulation with new noncombustible insulation.

(*18*) Recover/replace existing asphalt/vinyl asbestos tile with new VCT and provide new base (those areas which will not be carpeted); ramps, stairtreads/landings shall be raised orbital rubber tile.

(*19*) Carpet administrative offices, media center, all classrooms, teacher lounges, and small group study spaces. Provide new base throughout and "Pro-Gym" carpet in gym.

(*20*) Provide acoustical wall Tectum panels in cafeteria and gym (10′ A.F.F. in gym and 7′ A.F.F. in cafeteria).

(*21*) Recover chalk and tackboards throughout.

(*22*) Provide new solid plastic toilet partitions; all toilet stalls shall be floor-mounted and overhead-braced.

(*23*) Provide electrical hand dryers in gang toilets.

(*24*) Replace missing or damaged toilet accessories in all toilets, both gang and individual.

(*25*) Verify condition of venetian blinds and replace the ones damaged, missing, etc. Any new windows shall be provided with venetian blinds.

(*26*) Replace two-compartment sink in kitchen with three-compartment sink with booster heater in right side compartment. Survey condition of existing kitchen equipment, replace as required.

(*27*) Provide power for kiln and exhaust fan for kiln ventilation.

(*28*) Submit plans and specifications to State for approval and to Design and Construction for review and community/PTA presentation.

Plumbing

(*1*) Provide sprinkler system for the entire building as required by Fire Marshal, per Fairfax County Public Schools design criteria. The system shall be totally designed.

(*2*) Survey restrooms; replace fixtures, accessories, and valves as necessary. Replace all flush valves, faucets, and water closet seats, and bolt cap covers.

(*3*) Provide handicap fixtures in gang toilets, one on each floor, per Fairfax County Public Schools mounting height standards.

(*4*) All new toilet rooms are to have floor drains. Replace missing existing floor drain accessories.

(*5*) Provide tempered hot water, 110°F maximum, to all existing and new sinks. Tempering valves shall be thermostatic and pressure sensitive.

(*6*) Provide separate domestic water heating system (in addition to boiler system).

(*7*) Replace D.F. with E.W.C. Provide handicapped and standard heights per Fairfax County Public Schools mounting height standards.

(*8*) Provide hose bib at loading dock, if none exists.

(*9*) Add additional roof drains, if necessary. Replace existing roof drains as necessary.

(*10*) Field survey entire building to determine existing conditions and provide recommendations. Also review maintenance "wish list."

(*11*) Replace all valves on domestic water systems. Remove and replace any galvanized steel domestic water piping.

(*12*) Provide isolation valves on branch mains and for project phasing.

(*13*) Modify existing rough-ins for fixture changes, handicapped requirements, Fairfax County Public Schools mounting height standards, and drinking fountain replacement with E.W.C.

(*14*) New handicapped toilet rooms with single lavatory and water closet shall be a minimum of 5′6″ wide.

(*15*) Coordinate rough-ins and flush valves with handicapped grab bars.

Mechanical

(*1*) Upgrade the entire heating and cooling system to provide a twenty-year life expectancy.

(*2*) Completely air condition the entire building. (Some areas may already have air conditioning.) Replace existing air conditioning systems.

(*3*) Air condition design shall be based on ASHRAE standards, twenty-five students per classroom and minimum outside air per BOCA code. Design heat to 72°F and cool to 75°F.

(*4*) Inspect boilers, associated pumps, trims, etc. Recommend repairs (test boilers). Convert to dual fuel (IRI) oil/gas burners.

(*5*) Field survey entire building to determine existing conditions and provide recommendations. Also review maintenance "wish list."

(*6*) Submit future and existing heating load to Washington Gas.
(*7*) Provide additional ventilation for specialized spaces (kiln, etc.).
(*8*) Submit energy envelope calculations (new construction).
(*9*) Check existing roof top equipment to remain, repair, or replace.
(*10*) Provide DDC/pneumatic temperature control system (base bid) per Fairfax County Public Schools design criteria.
(*11*) Replace existing fuel oil system completely including piping per Fairfax County Public Schools design criteria.
(*12*) Replace all heating or cooling system valves.
(*13*) Provide isolation valves for project phasing and for any branch lines serving three units or more.
(*14*) Coordinate for provisions for screening rooftop air conditioning equipment.
(*15*) Design shall comply with Fairfax County Public Schools design criteria, guide specifications, and typical details furnished.

Electrical

(*1*) New electric services as required.
(*2*) Upgrade lighting in accordance with Illumination Engineering Society standards and Virginia Department of Education.
(*3*) Upgrade TV system for cable, new antennas, and head-end equipment. Provide TV outlets in classrooms, gym, and lunch room (if not already there).
(*4*) Add electrical outlets (minimum four per classroom).
(*5*) Upgrade PA console and auxiliary sound system.
(*6*) Install new fire alarm system with graphic annunciator panel. Provide smoke detectors in corridors, library, office, cafeteria. Provide heat detectors in janitor' s closet, boiler room, kitchen, etc.
(*7*) Provide security system on all exterior doors, administration, media, kitchen, cafeteria, computer rooms.
(*8*) Upgrade program clock system.
(*9*) Provide power for relocated art kiln.
(*10*) Provide all additional power for air conditioning and elevator.
(*11*) Connect telephone sound, fire alarm, emergency lights, exit lights, security light, and sound console, to emergency power source (verify capacity).

(*12*) Provide contactor control on exterior lighting for future connection to Computer Controlled Management System.

(*13*) Provide central contactor control or ventilation equipment for connection to Computer Controlled Management System.

(*14*) Replace/modify existing power distribution and branch circuit wiring.

(*15*) Evaluate, modify, and upgrade site and security lighting.

RFP Evaluation Criteria

RFP EVALUATION CRITERIA

The School Board of the City of Newport News is interested in receiving proposals from qualified architectural and engineering firms licensed in Virginia for professional services required to renovate the existing 175,000 square foot school building located at 6060 Jefferson Avenue. Proposals will be evaluated based on the following criteria:

1. Prior experience in the design of school facilities and in large renovation projects which include extensive mechanical-electrical upgrades and replacement of roofing which contains asbestos. (30%)
2. Understanding of the procedures to be followed with the State Department of Education for approval of plans and specifications. (10%)
3. The quality of prior work in planning, design, measured drawing, construction documents and contract administration. (20%)
4. Profiles of the personnel and the project team within the firm and its consultants to include prior experience in designing education facilities, renovations, mechanical-electrical replacements and removing roofing with asbestos. (10%)
5. Ability to perform these projects on time (measured drawings, planning, design, cost estimating, construction documents and construction administration). (15%)
6. Ability to be at the project site on a daily basis if necessary or as required by the School Board. (10%)
7. Demonstrated commitment to equal employment opportunities, affirmative action and minority business participation. (5%)

Three (3) copies of these proposals to be submitted to Dr. Wayne D. Lett, Assistant Superintendent for Business, 12465 Warwick Boulevard, Newport News, Virginia, 23606-0130, no later than 2:00 p.m., November 25, 1992. The School Board reserves the right to reject any and all proposals and to award this contract in whole or in part.

Dr. Eric J. Smith
Division Superintendent

WRITTEN PROPOSAL EVALUATION

PROJECT: A/E SERVICES FOR RENOVATION OF MIDDLE SCHOOL

FIRM NAME: ____________________

EVALUATOR NAME: ____________________

DATE OF EVALUATION: ____________________

PROCEDURES: Each Evaluator shall privately review the proposal submitted by the above firm. Enter the score for each criteria as follows:

O = failed to demonstrate capability.

MAXIMUM = Demonstrated exactly the capability requested.

Total your scores at the bottom of this sheet, put one sheet for each proposal in an envelope and give to Dr. Lett or Leah Lively. Do not discuss your results with the other evaluators until all scores are published.

#	CRITERIA	MAXIMUM POSSIBLE	SCORE
1	Prior Experience of Firm	30	
2	Understand VDOE Procedure	10	
3	Quality of Prior Work	20	
4	Project Team Experience	10	
5	Ability to Perform on Time	15	
6	Ability to be On-Site Daily	10	
7	Past Commitment to E.E.O. & MBP	5	
	TOTAL	100	

Name of Firm ________________________ Evaluator __________________

RENOVATION A/E SELECTION INTERVIEW

	(Each question has a maximum value of 4 points)	Points Awarded
1.	What impact will the new BOCA Code and the Americans with Disabilities Act have on the feasibility and cost of this renovation?	
2.	How can we balance first costs with life-cycle costs when we upgrade the mechanical and electrical systems and replace window systems and exterior doors in this school?	
3.	What type of roof replacement system will be most cost effective for us?	
4.	What are the advantages and disadvantages of prequalifying general contractors?	
5.	How can we ensure compatibility with our existing Network 8000 Barber Coleman EMCS (15 schools) and get competitive HVAC control prices?	
6.	How can you best control the quality of your programming, design and documentation to obtain competitive bids from qualified bidders?	
7.	How can you assure the school division that your product selection and specifications will assure cost effectiveness with your desire to be esthetically pleasing?	
8.	What percentage of the base bid estimate should be reserved for general contract change orders for this renovation?	
9.	What is the impact of the physical facility on learning, morale and discipline?	
10.	Which members of your project team will we actually be dealing with on a daily basis during this project?	
11.	What are the credentials of these team members which make your team significantly more capable of providing our services than your competitors?	
12.	What do you consider to be the weaknesses of your team?	
13.	What level of site observation do you recommend for the contract administration phase of this renovation?	
14.	How will you respond if the general contractors' poor performance necessitates frequent or daily visits to ensure conformance with the contract documents?	
15.	How do you propose to provide business opportunities to minority businesses?	
	Subtotal	
	Presentation (Maximum Value 40 points)	
	Total	

AGREEMENT

BETWEEN

OWNER AND CONTRACTOR
Monroe County Schools

Agreement

made as of the *sixth* day of *March* in the year Nineteen Hundred and *Ninety-four.*

BETWEEN THE OWNER: *Monroe County Schools*
Monroe City, Virginia

and the CONTRACTOR: *Potomac Contractors, Inc.*

The Project: *Renovation of the Monroe County High School Elm Street and Hamilton Avenue*

The Architect: *Smith and Jones, Architects, Inc.*

The Owner and the Contractor agree as set forth below.

Article 1
The Contract Documents

The Contract Documents consist of this Agreement, the Conditions of the Contract (General Supplementary and other Conditions), the Architectural Drawings, the Technical Specifications, all Addenda issued prior to and all Modifications issued after execution of this Agreement. These documents form the Contract, and all are as fully a part of the contract as if attached to this Agreement or repeated herein. An enumeration of the Contract Documents appears in Article 7.

Article 2
The Work

The Contractor shall perform all the Work required by the Contract Documents for *the renovation of the existing Monroe County High School.*

Article 3
Time of Commencement and Substantial Completion

The work to be performed under this Contract shall be commenced and, subject to authorized adjustments, Substantial Completion shall be achieved not later than *Twelve (12) months from the date of this contract.*

Article 4
Contract Sum

The Owner shall pay the Contractor in current funds for the performance of the work, subject to additions and deductions by Change Order as provided in the Contract Documents, the Contract Sum of *$8,568,000.*

The Contract sum is determined as follows:

Article 5
Progress Payments

Based upon Applications for Payment submitted to the Architect by the Contractor and Certificates for Payment issued by the Architect, the Owner shall make progress payments on account of the Contract Sum to the Contractor as provided in the Contract Documents for the period ending the *fifth* day of the month as follows: *beginning with April 5, 1995.*

Not later than ______ days following the end of the period covered by the Application for Payment ____ percent (__%) of the portion of the Contract Sum properly allocable to labor, materials, and equipment incorporated in the Work and ____ percent (__%) of the portion of the Contract Sum properly allocable to materials and equipment suitably stored at the site or at some other location agreed upon in writing, for the period covered by the Application for Payment, less the aggregate of previous payments made by the Owner; and upon substantial Completion of the entire work, a sum sufficient to increase the total payments to ____ percent (__%) of the Contract Sum, less such amounts as the Architect shall determine for all incomplete work and unsettled claims as provided in the Contract Documents.

Article 6
Final Payment

Final payment, constituting the entire unpaid balance of the contract Sum, shall be paid by the Owner to the Contractor when the work has been completed, the contract fully performed, and a final Certificate for Payments has been issued by the Architect.

Article 7
Miscellaneous Provisions

7.1 Terms used in this Agreement which are defined in the Conditions of the Contract shall have the meanings designated in those Conditions.
7.2 The Contract Documents, which constitute the entire agreement between the Owner and the Contractor, as listed in Article 1 and, except for Modifications issued after execution of this Agreement, are enumerated as follows:

This agreement entered into as of the day and year first written above.

OWNER CONTRACTOR

____

____

____

____

Position Description

POSITION TITLE

Construction Supervisor

EFFECTIVE DATE

July 1, 1991

REPORTS TO

Director of Construction

QUALIFICATIONS

A degree in engineering/engineering related field preferred, or comparable experience in design and construction and five years experience involving planning, design, and supervision of construction activities.

STATE REQUIREMENTS/QUALIFICATIONS

None

BASIC FUNCTION

Performance of construction management activities in the planning, design, construction of educational facilities.

DIMENSIONS

Budget responsibilities: None
Employees supervised: None

DUTIES AND RESPONSIBILITIES:

This position encompasses coordination of activities and resolution of problems among contractor-supervisory personnel, architect/engineers, School Board Staff, and governmental officials concerning technical matters related to building foundations, structures, mechanical systems, electrical and communications systems, grading, paving, and drainage. Resolving problems concerning scheduling and coordinating diverse construction activities.

This position requires comprehensive knowledge of standards and procedures for planning, design, scheduling, and quality control of school building programs.

Represents the owner on construction project sites by administering contracts between the School Board and general contractors, separate contractors, and architect/engineers.

Consults with representatives of governmental agencies, School Board staff architects, contractors, and other interested officials to resolve problems concerning interpretation of contract documents.

Establishes coordination and procedural policies for project accomplishment.

Conducts pre-construction conferences and weekly job site meetings. Resolves on-going construction site problems.

Establishes and maintains a continuous quality control program to assure that facilities are constructed to acceptable standards.

Directs improvement in standards of work.

Approves quality of completed work.

Determines adequacy of and recommends approval of payment requests.

Assesses work progress and scheduling and recommends actions for improvement.

Prepares progress reports and maintains project records.

Reviews and approves shop drawings, product data and samples.

Observes testing procedures, reviews test and inspection reports and expenditures corrective action.

Determines the need for contract changes, make recommendations for accomplishment of the change and processes change orders.

Directors installation and inspection of owner furnished equipment and material.

Directors the work of separate contractors.

Conducts final inspections with contractors and architects/engineers.

Coordinates project acceptance, building occupation, and start-up educational activities with staff and governmental agencies.

Coordinates the orientation of maintenance and operational personnel on school plant operation.

Supervises contractor activity during the guarantee period.

Reviews and verifies project closeout documents, as-built drawings, operation manuals, and project releases.

Assists in the development of contract specifications and contract documents.

Reviews architect/engineer submissions for preliminary, intermediate, and final design stages and makes recommendations for design changes.

Assists in the coordination of design review by appropriate governmental agencies.

Coordinates new facilities requirements with the staff.

Prepares cost estimates.

Provides architect/engineer with design parameters including minimum standards and building systems (type, size, model, quality, etc.).

Prepares design and construction schedules.

Makes recommendations on construction procedures and contracting methods.